GW00632971

Images 24

the best of British illustration

RotoVision

Images 24 published by Rotovision SA
Rue Du Bugnon 7
CH-1299 Crans-Près-Céligny
Switzerland

Exhibitions and Events Manager &
Images Editor: Emily Glass
Telephone: +44 (0)20 7733 2955

Book Design: Nicole Griffin

Production in Singapore by
ProVision Pte. Ltd.
Telephone: +65 334 7720
Fax: +65 334 7721

All rights reserved. No part of this book
may be produced in any form or by any
electronic or mechanical means including
information storage and retrieval systems
without permission in writing from the
Publisher, except by a reviewer who may
quote brief passages in a review. This
book is sold subject to the condition
that it shall not be distributed by way
of trade or otherwise be circulated
without the Publisher's prior consent.
All transparencies and/or illustrations
reproduced in the book have been
accepted on the condition that they are
reproduced with the knowledge and prior
consent of the illustrator concerned and
no responsibility is accepted by the
Publisher or Printer for any infringement
of copyright or otherwise arising out of
publication thereof. The work of this
annual is the choice of the Artists and/or
their representatives, not of the publisher.
As this book is printed in four-colour
process, a few of the illustrations
reproduced here may appear to be
slightly different than in their original
reproduction.

All illustrations and text published in
Images 24 have been submitted by the
artists or the client company. Work
featured within the various categories was
chosen by a jury appointed by the AOI.
The publisher therefore cannot accept any
responsibility or liability for any
infringement of copyright or otherwise
arising out of the publication thereof.

The information published on the
illustrators featured must not be used to
compile either mailing lists or any other
directories or publications. Any
unauthorised use of the information
contained in this book will lead to
immediate legal proceedings.

Copyright © RotoVision and
The Association of Illustrators 2000

ISBN 2-88046-476-5

Rotovision SA
Editorial & Sales Office
Sheridan House
112/116A Western Road
Hove BN3 1DD
England
Tel: +44 (0)1273 72 72 68
Fax: +44 (0)1273 72 72 69
E-mail: sales@RotoVision.com
Website: www.RotoVision.com

Association of Illustrators
1-5 Beehive Place
London SW9 7QR
Tel: +44 (0)20 7733 5844
Fax: +44 (0)20 7733 1199
E-mail: info@a-o-illustrators.demon.co.uk
Website: www.aoi.co.uk

Acknowledgements
We are grateful for the support of many
organisations and individuals who
contributed to the *Images* Exhibition and
annual as follows:
- Our 27 judges on the judging panel for
  applying their expertise to the difficult
  task of selecting this year's work
- The Royal College of Art for hosting
  the Images 24 exhibition
- Moshe Gerstenhaber and Nigel Toplis
  at Kall Kwik for sponsoring the AOI/Kall
  Kwik Illustrator Award and Kall Kwik
  Print and Design Award
- Waterstone's Booksellers, Winsor &
  Newton, Transworld Publishers Ltd,
  Pentagram Design Ltd, Hawkins
  Innovation Network and Daler Rowney
  for their generosity in sponsoring
  awards for *Images* 24
- Jill Calder for the use of her illustration
  on the Call for Entry form
- Stephens Innocent Solicitors for their
  legal advice
- Nicole Harman, Jackie Rye, Gary French
  and Simon Hennessey for the
  production of Images 24
- All our volunteers for their invaluable
  assistance with the competition and
  exhibition
- AOI Manager Samantha Taylor
- AOI Managing Council: Ali Pellatt
  (chair), Francis Blake, Michael Bramman,
  Derek Brazell, Stuart Briers, Joanne
  Davies, Adam Graff and James Marsh
- Nicole Griffin for her design

Contents

Foreword

By Ali Pellatt/AOI Chair

Well, what a year. For some time there has been a rumble in the jungle that illustration was ready to pounce again after a few years licking its wounds since the recession. It seems that every time I turned on the TV, glanced up at a billboard or opened a newspaper yet another original and clever illustration beamed back. Exciting and innovative work was in abundance in 1999. Congratulations to all those illustrators and to the commissioners and clients whose creative juices have been running wild.

With a nod towards the millennium, the AOI's seminar, 'The Future of Illustration', capitalised on our image maker's recent return to popularity musing the dramatic role that technology has had to play in all this. Even illustrators using traditional media have turned to the computer for faster execution of artwork and speedier communication with clients. Some of the most exciting illustration is computer generated and Henry Obasi, the AOI/Kall Kwik Award winner exemplifies the best of British illustration in this field.

Hopefully, his success will encourage other ground-breaking illustrators to enter Images 25 and motivate more clients to take risks with the many new and varied illustrators around today.

It is becoming increasingly important for commissioners to access your portfolio on the net. Subscribing to the AOI's website is an excellent way to reach new clients. Costs are low and you can update material regularly. To add to the prestige of the site we have now included the whole of Images 24.

So, all eyes on the future. Our sub-committees for education, sponsorship and Images are proving to be highly successful. We are reaching out to more students, appreciating increased support from illustrator friendly businesses and are already on the way to creating a bigger and better Images competition for 2000.

Enjoy Images 24 and may good fortune and dream commissions come your way.

Images 24 tour
Tour venues will include:
Royal College of Art, London
European Illustration Collection, Hull
mac, Birmingham
Suffolk College, Ipswich

Introduction to the AOI

The AOI was established in 1973 to advance and protect illustrators' rights and encourage professional standards. The AOI is a non-profit making trade association dedicated to its members' professional interests and the promotion of illustration.

Members consist primarily of freelance illustrators as well as agents, clients, students and lecturers. The AOI is run by an administrative staff responsible to a Council of Management.

As the only body to represent illustrators and campaign for their rights in the UK, the AOI has successfully increased the standing of illustration as a profession and improved the commercial and ethical conditions of employment for illustrators.

Campaigning

The AOI is a member of the British Copyright Council and the Creators Copyright Coalition. It helped set up the secondary rights arm of DACS, the UK visual arts collecting society.

The AOI was responsible for establishing the right of illustrators to retain ownership of their artwork and continues to campaign against loss of copyright control, bad contracts and exploitative practices. We will expose companies who consistently abuse illustrators' rights.

Information and support services

Portfolio advice

Members are entitled to a free annual consultation with the AOI's portfolio consultant. Objective advice is given on portfolio presentation and content, suitable illustration markets and agents.

Journal

The AOI Journal (**Illustrator**) is distributed monthly to members, keeping them informed about exhibitions, competitions, campaigns and activities in the profession.

Hotline advice

Members have access to a special Hotline number if they need advice about pricing commissions, copyright and ethics problems.

Publications

The AOI publishes **Rights: The Illustrator's Guide to Professional Practice** a comprehensive guide to the law for illustrators. It provides detailed advice on how to protect against exploitative practices and contains a model contract for illustrators to use. We also produce **Survive: The Illustrator's Guide to a professional Career** which is a comprehensive practical guide to beginning and continuing a career as a professional illustrator. **Survive** includes information about marketing, ethics, agents and a guide to fees. These publications are available to members at reduced rates.

Client directories

The AOI currently has three illustration client directories which are only available for purchase by members. The **Editorial Directory** has details of over 120 contacts in the newspaper and magazine industries. The **Publishing Directory** is a comprehensive list of important contacts in book publishing. The **Advertising Directory** has details of over 150 contacts from the world of advertising.

Business advice

Members are entitled to a free consultation with the AOI Chartered Accountant, who can advise on accounting, National Insurance, tax, VAT and book-keeping.

Regional groups

The contact details of regional representatives are available to members who organise social activities for regional members and provide an important support network.

Discounts

Members receive discounts on a range of services, including a number of art material suppliers nationwide.

Legal advice

Full members receive advice on ethics and contractual problems, copyright and moral right disputes.

Return of artwork stickers

Available to AOI members only. These stickers help safeguard the return of artwork.

Students & new illustrators

Our seminars and events, combined with the many services we offer, can provide practical support to illustrators in the early stages of their career.

Image file

Members can promote their work to clients visiting the AOI office via the *Image File* containing copies of members' work.

Events

The AOI runs an annual programme of events which include one day seminars, evening lectures and thematic exhibitions. These cover subjects such as talks by leading illustrators, children's book illustration, aspects of professional practice, new technologies and illustrators' agents. AOI members are entitled to discounted tickets.

To request further information or a membership application form please telephone +44 (0)20 7733 5844.

ASSOCIATION OF
ILLUSTRATORS

The AOI patrons

JANET WOOLLEY

RAYMOND BRIGGS

BRIAN GRIMWOOD

SIMON STERN

CHLOE CHEESE

IAN POLLOCK

RONALD SEARLE

Raymond Briggs

Raymond Briggs was born in 1934. He studied painting at Wimbledon School of Art and the Slade School and has been illustrating since 1957 and writing since 1961. His best known books include *Father Christmas*, 1973, *Fungus the Bogeyman*, 1977, *The Snowman*, 1979, and *When the Wind Blows*, 1982 (book, radio play, stage play and feature film). His most recent work, a strip-cartoon biography of his parents *Ethel and Earnest* has also become a best seller.

Simon Stern

Born and brought up in North London, where he still lives, Simon Stern worked as a graphic designer for ten years before turning to illustration. He has done just about everything from children's books to (briefly) political cartoons for the Times Saturday Review, and currently works mostly as an editorial and advertising illustrator. Since helping his step daughter with her law degree, he has made a special study of legal issues associated with illustration, and wrote the AOI handbook *Rights*. He takes part in a number of industry bodies which aim to protect the rights of creators, and is a director of DACS, the visual arts collecting society. He has been a member of the AOI since 1975 and believes it to be a vital organisation in a period when many illustrators are having a hard time, facing rights grabs from clients as well as the threat to their livelihood presented by stock imagery.

Ronald Searle

Ronald Searle, apart from founding St. Trinian's and co-fathering Nigel Molesworth, has been a freelance illustrator for more years than he cares to reflect on. He has been a special correspondent for Life Magazine, cover artist and long-time contributor to the New Yorker Magazine and, currently, an editorial cartoonist to the French daily Le Monde. Over the years some fifty albums of his drawings have been published and regular exhibitions of his satirical graphic have been held in European and American museums. He is also a designer of commemorative medals for the French Mint and the British Art Medal Society. He has lived in France since 1961 and still does not regret it.

Ian Pollock

Pollock has been freelancing for a quarter of a century. 'Mostly editorial'. Born in 1950, son of Gordon Pollock, traditional clay pipe-manufacturer, he studied illustration at Manchester Polytechnic and the Royal College of Art. He now lives in Macclesfield. He was commissioned to design a set of four postage stamps – 'Tales of Terror' – for the Royal Mail which were issued in May 1997.

'I occasionally get the old buzz, but not often . . . too many roughs spoil the broth.' He said reaching for another slug pellet. 'Want one?'

Janet Woolley

Janet Woolley has been a freelance illustrator since 1976 when she left the Royal College of Art. Janet works in the areas of editorial and advertising illustration in Europe and the USA, and is a Visiting Professor of Illustration at Central Saint Martin's College of Art.

Brian Grimwood

Brian Grimwood has been credited by Print magazine as having changed the look of British illustration. He has worked for most of the major publications in the UK and Europe and has become one of Britain's most innovative and influential illustrators.

In 1983 he co-founded the Central Illlustration Agency that now represents 45 of London's most prestigious illustrators.

As well as exhibiting in numerous group shows, he has had six one-man shows.

Chloe Cheese

I left the RCA in 1976 and since then, although at first almost obsessed with drawing food and still life subjects, I have gradually explored different media and themes.

At the moment I find the imaginative freedom that is part of children's book illustration gives me great pleasure in my work.

Tony Ross

Oh dear, it's that time of year again, when I must think of something to say at the beginning of the annual. It's always difficult, because my sort of illustration is a pretty uncomplicated affair. Thinking back though, it's not always been so. When I taught illustration, a lot of my students' day to day problems, (and mine) were rapidly sorted out by the AOI. So . . . students, teachers, make contact. Entering our business can be a spooky experience, and sometimes I wonder if students are aware of the help we can give. It might be good to know more about you, than to simply tell you about us, after all, the friendlier we are, the stronger we are.

Go on, spoil yourselves, take advantage, say 'Hello'.

Glen Baxter

Glen Baxter was born in the tiny Northern hamlet of Hunslet. After a series of educational errors he was removed and installed in a crumbling Victorian manor house in Camberwell, where his condition is said to be 'almost stable.'

He is the author of *The Impending Gleam*, *Cranireons ov Botya*, *The Wonder Book of Sex* and *Glen Baxter's Gourmet Guide*.

His drawings have been exhibited in Paris, New York, Venice, Tokyo, Sydney, Amsterdam and Ikley. Forthcoming exhibitions for '98-'99 include the Modernism Gallery, San Francisco, Galerie de la Chatre, Paris and a retrospective at the French National Print Center.

Quentin Blake

Quentin Blake read English at Cambridge University, and Education at London University, before becoming a part-time student at Chelsea School of Art and a full-time freelance illustrator simultaneously, just about 40 years ago. He taught in the illustration department of the Royal College of Art, which he ran for several years.

His recent work includes John Yeoman's *Up with the Birds!* and an illustrated edition of *The Hunchback of Notre Dame* for the Folio Society, as well as two books of his own, *The Green Ship* and *Zagazoo*.

Ralph Steadman

Ralph Steadman became a freelance cartoonist and illustrator after attending the London College of Printing and Graphic Arts in the early 1960s, working for *Punch*, *Private Eye*, *The Telegraph*, *New York Times* and *Rolling Stone Magazine*.

He has written and illustrated books on Sigmund Freud, Leonardo Da Vinci, *The Big I Am* (the story of creation and its aftermath), and *Tales of The Wieirrd* (a collection of eccentrics and obsessive characters in history). He has illustrated *Alice in Wonderland*, *Alice Through The Looking Glass* and *The Hunting of The Snark*, *Treasure Island*, the works of Flann O'Brien and, most recently, the anniversary edition of *Animal Farm* in 1995.

Having travelled the world's vineyards and distilleries for Oddbins, he has illustrated and written two books of his journeys – *Grapes of Ralph* and *Still Life With Bottle*.

For the past few years he has been working on a series of etchings and silkscreen prints exploring the theme of 'leaders and writers' with Peacock Printmakers, Aberdeen. These works have been exhibited in Aberdeen, Denver and Aspen in the US.

In 1987, Ralph Steadman was the recipient of the W.H. Smith Illustration Award for the best illustrated book of the past five years (for *I Leonardo*) and the BBC Design Award for postage stamps. He also won the Italian Critica in Erba Prize and the Black Humour Award in France. He is a Fellow of the Kent Institute of Art and design, and in 1995 was awarded an Hon.D.Litt. by the University of Kent.

Peter Blake

I am very proud to be the only artist who is both a Royal Academician as a painter and a Royal Designer to Industry as an illustrator.

Carolyn Gowdy

Carolyn Gowdy was born in Seattle, USA, studied at the University of Washington, Seattle, Rhode Island School of Design, Providence and the Royal College of Art, London, leaving in 1980.

This year four paintings were commissioned for an especially inspired advertising campaign. Then, like a curious theatre of dreams, they appeared in enormous format across the whole of London Underground and beyond.

Meanwhile, she was invited to exhibit in Tel Aviv, to show and tell stories about her work in Florence and Oslo, as well as teaching illustration in Copenhagen. Her heart continues to sing.

Shirley Hughes

Shirley Hughes began freelancing as an illustrator in the 1950s. Her picture books for young children, featuring characters like 'Dogger' and 'Alfie', are now reaching a second generation both here and abroad, reflecting an affectionate and unsentimental picture of the joys and dramas of family life. Recently she has also produced some visually inventive stories for slightly older children.

Illustration is from 'Enchantment in the Garden' written and illustrated by Shirley Hughes.

QUENTIN BLAKE

SHIRLEY HUGHES

TONY ROSS

GLEN BAXTER

ROBIN NOTICED THE PROBLEM
ALMOST IMMEDIATELY

RALPH STEADMAN

CAROLYN GOWDY

PETER BLAKE

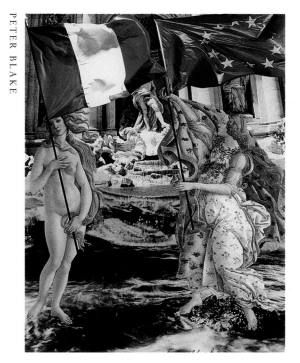

The AOI/Kall Kwik Illustrator Award

Award winner: Henry Obasi

Interview by Ali Pellatt/AOI Chair

Dear Illustrator

We at Kall Kwik are very proud to continue our relationship with the Association of Illustrators through the annual awards and *Images 24*.

This is the third year that we have been involved with the AOI and to our mind there is tremendous synergy between the two organisations, the two brands and most importantly the mindsets of each.

We have built our Company on the foundation stones of consistent high quality, exceptional service and an empathy with customers.

To do this has required not just hard work and know-how but imagination, creativity and a certain level of skill – but most importantly it has shown that to be successful in this field you need to be passionate about serving people's needs in a way that really delights them.

These skills and attributes are in my mind very similar to those of the illustrator – that is creativity, passion, perserverance and hard work. Plus of course the all important need to know your customer.

Once again we wish you well.

Nigel Toplis

Joint Managing Director

Kall Kwik

Henry Obasi began training as a civil engineer before abandoning his course in favour of an Arts degree. After completing his foundation at Chelsea he graduated from the London College of Printing in 1997 having studied graphics, specialisng in screen printing. Even at LCP he veered off from the simplest, straightest path. This time towards illustration after his tutors, Tony Braithwaite, Paul Bowman and the late Paul Eckersley, saw his talents and nudged him in the right direction. After graduation he lugged his portfolio around alongside all the other Good, Bad and Uglies from college and landed the Firetrap job almost by chance. Success exploded into Henry's life like a time bomb in an ink factory.

His winning Images entry 'Stagnight' was one of a series of four illustrations commissioned by Fold 7 for Firetrap. Henry literally arrived at the eleventh hour on a regular portfolio visit as the designers were all set to commission another illustrator. Originally they were looking for a fairly popular scratchy, inky style. It was nearly in the bag. Then, stepping back in to the office after a spot of lunch, they spied Henry with his portfolio and the rest is illustration history.

Within two weeks he had presented six finished pieces of artwork for the pitch. Very few changes were made from the rough stage, almost none at all for 'Stagnight'. Four were chosen and a couple of months later the images were being shown in print, animation and installations in two European fashion trade shows. His images were blasted over sheets of canvas, projected onto walls and used on CD covers to promote the company.

At the time of interview Henry was working almost exclusively for Fold 7, expanding his style and blurring the boundaries between graphics, animation and illustration. As a result of this high profile campaign Mac User commissioned him to do a cover and since then his client list has gone off the Richter scale. Henry is currently studying for an MA at Central St Martins as well as working for clients such as Mercedes, EMI, Mother, Springer and Jacoby International.

For some time now the AOI has been especially keen to support the eclectic use of imagery in illustration. Henry's fluid, buzzy work perfectly epitomises the maverick spirit of invention which is paving the way for futher exciting, ground-breaking illustrations of the future.

Images 24 award winners

 ### The AOI/Kall Kwik Illustrator Award

Henry Obasi: *Stag Night*
Awarded to the illustrator with the highest overall marks from the judging panel.

 ### The Kall Kwik Print & Design Award

Sara Fanelli: *Millennium Stamp*
Awarded to the illustrator with the highest marks from the judging panel in the Print & Design section.

 ### AOI Client Award

Sian Lewis of the *Saturday Express* magazine for:
Marie Antoinette by Paul Slater
Awarded to the commissioning editor who submitted illustrations which received the highest marks from the judging panel.

 ### Pentagram Award

Ceri Amphlett: *You Half Turn into a Zebra*
Roderick Mills: *Riding with the Sun*
Paul Wearing: *Finnegans Wake*
These artists have been selected by Pentagram Design Ltd for an exhibition at their gallery in Notting Hill, London.

 ### Waterstone's Booksellers Award

Roman Pisarev: *The Count of Monte Cristo*
Awarded to the illustrator with the
highest marks from the judging panel in the
General Books section.

 ### The Transworld Children's Book Award

Alison Jay: *Picture This*
Awarded to the illustrator with the highest marks from the judging panel in the Children's Book section.

 ### Hawkins Innovation Network Student Award

Jonathon Cusick: *Knit One, Pearl Two*
Awarded to the illustrator with the highest marks from the judging panel in the Student section.

 ### The Daler-Rowney Award

Michael Bramman: *A Little Tram Music*
Awarded to the illustrator for the best use of traditional materials

 ### The Winsor & Newton Award

Liz Minichiello: *St Martin's Place*
Awarded to the illustrator for the best use of traditional materials

HENRY OBASI

JONATHON CUSICK

MICHAEL BRAMMAN

LIZ MINICHIELLO

SARA FANELLI

PAUL SLATER

RODERICK MILLS

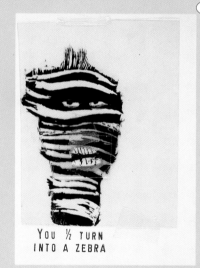

PAUL WEARING

YOU ½ TURN
INTO A ZEBRA

CERI AMPHLETT

ROMAN PISAREV

ALISON JAY

IMAGES 24 AWARD WINNERS

judges

Janet Saville / Art Buyer / JWT

Simon Stern / Illustrator

Lindsay Wilton / Head Art Buyer / Saatchi & Saatchi

Peter Gausis / Art Director / Abbott Mead Vickers

Illustration by Frank Love +44 (0)20 8297 2212

advertising

AOI · KallKwik · PRINT COPY DESIGN

★ award winner: *The AOI Kall Kwik Illustrator Award*
★ **Highest mark in Images 24**

henry obasi

49 Clovelly Road
Chiswick
London
W4 5DU
t. 020 8995 9017
t. 020 7251 0101
f. 020 8995 9017
m. 07909 904 400
email. henry@fold7.co.uk

17
GB

title
Stag Night

medium
Pen, ink,
photography &
digital

purpose of work
Advertising Firetrap
clothing campaign
1999

brief
Raw edge

commissioned by
Steve Atkinson

company
'Fire Trap'

agent
Fold 7
56-58 Clerkenwell
Road
London
E1CM 5PX
t. 020 7251 0101
f. 020 7251 0202

diana fernando

The Old Post Office
18 The Street
Wissett
Suffolk
IP19 0JE

t. 01986 872087
f. 01986 872087

18
GB

The Two Sulphurs

The two aspects of Sulphur - volatile (winged griffin) and fixed (wingless lion) -
fight, then combine to allow transformation leading to Gold.

title
The Two Sulphurs

medium
Indian ink on
cream paper,
photographically
tinted and enlarged

purpose of work
Big Gold tinted
wall-print for
finance house
"Alchemy"

brief
To design and
produce traditional
looking alchemical
print of two lions
fighting
representing
transmutation into
gold to encourage
aggressive
bargaining in the
conference room

commissioned by
Jon Moulton

company
Alchemy Partners

adam graff

10 St. Columbas House
16 Prospect Hill
Upper Walthamstow
London
E17 3EZ

t. 020 8521 7182
f. 020 8521 7182
m. 07747 196 811
email. graff@st-columbus.demon.co.uk

title	**brief**
Fun Run	To illustrate the
medium	title "Fun Run"
Chinagraph /	**commissioned by**
Computer	Jane Deacon
purpose of work	**company**
Poster and entry	Shelter
form cover to	**agent**
advertise	The Organisation
sponsored fun run	69 Caledonian
for charity Shelter	Road
	London
	N1 9BT
	t. 020 7833 8268

andrew kingham

See Agent

title
Big Planet, Small World

medium
Metal

purpose of work
European advertising campaign for BASF Coatings AG

brief
To reflect the relationship of BASF with its global clients

commissioned by
Toni Neu

company
Borsch Stengel Korner Bozell

agent
The Inkshed
98 Columbia Road
London
E2 7QB
t. 020 7613 2323

title
Catching The Star

medium
Metal

purpose of work
European advertising campaign for BASF Coatings AG

brief
To reflect the desire of BASF to help its clients realise their ambitions

commissioned by
Toni Neu

company
Borsch Stengel Korner Bozell

agent
The Inkshed
98 Columbia Road
London
E2 7QB
t. 020 7613 2323

nick hardcastle

98 Eaton road
Norwich
Norfolk
NR4 6PR
t. 01603 452855
f. 01603 452855

title
Satellite Dish
medium
Pen and ink with
watercolour
purpose of work
Trade advertising
for Shell Marine
brief
To illustrate the
copy line "Isn't it
time you had a
data transmission
service you can
afford"

commissioned by
Martin Mahler
company
Publicis
agent
Illustrators.Co
3 Richbourne
Terrace
London
SW8 1AR
t. 020 7793 7000

title
Large Ship and
Small Boat
medium
Pen and ink with
watercolour
purpose of work
Trade advertising
for Shell Marine
brief
To illustrate the
copy line "Now you
can afford to get
ahead with the hi-
tech revolution
whatever size you
are"

commissioned by
Martin Mahler
company
Publicis
agent
Illustrators.Co
3 Richbourne
Terrace
London
SW8 1AR
t. 020 7793 7000

james marsh

21 Elms Road
London
SW4 9ER

t. 020 7622 9530
f. 020 7498 6851

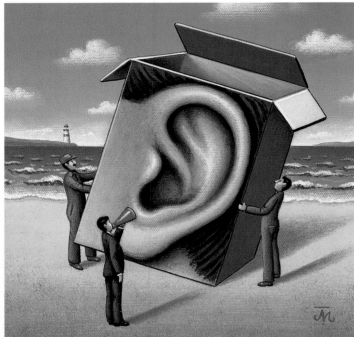

title
Background

brief
To illustrate the
theme of
background
information

title
Case Studies

brief
To illustrate the
theme of case
studies

title
Warehousing

brief
To illustrate the
theme of
warehousing
logistics

medium
Acrylics on canvas

purpose of work
Part of a series of
6 for a Parcel Force
promotion

commissioned by
Steve Coelho

company
Craik Jones

150 Curtain Road
Back Building
1st Floor Studio
London
EC2A 3AT

t. 020 7613 4434
f. 020 7613 4434
m. 0973 616054
email. frazer@dircon.co.uk

23

GB

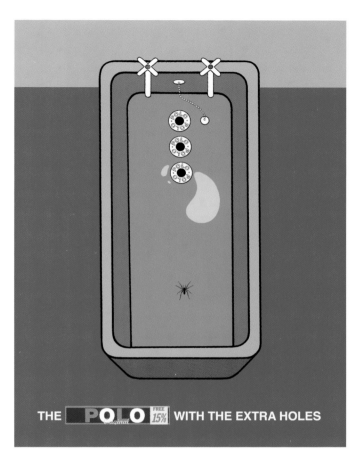

THE **POLO** FREE 15% WITH THE EXTRA HOLES

title
"Polo Bath"

medium
Computer
generated from
scanned drawings

purpose of work
Full page national
press ads to
promote 15% extra
polos in packets

brief
Produce three
concept
illustrations
promoting the idea
of 15% extra polo
mints in each new
packet. The
imagery should
have a minimal
look and the colour
scheme should be
cool and minty

commissioned by
Ken Grimshaw

company
J. Walter Thompson

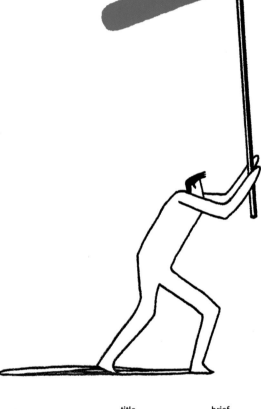

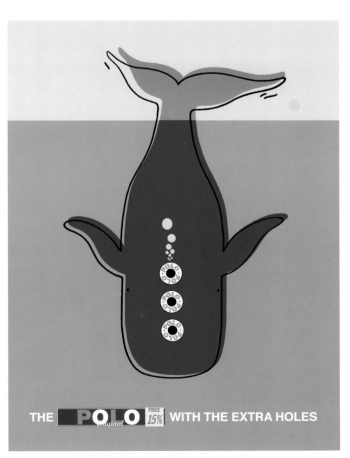

THE **POLO** FREE 15% WITH THE EXTRA HOLES

title
"Polo Whale"

title
Building our Brand
on the Web

medium
Computer
generated from
scanned drawings

purpose of work
Concept
illustrations to
advertise Ericsson's
Intranet site and
brochure

brief
Develop a series of
line drawings
summarising
Ericsson's brand
stewardship and
using company
colours. The
drawings should be
effective in their
simplicity and
easily transferred
for Intranet use

commissioned by
Stuart Jane

company
Imagination

michael sheehy

115 Crystal Palace
Road
East Dulwich
London
SE22 9ES

t. 020 8693 4315
f. 020 8693 4315

24

GB

title
Fibre Optics in the
City

medium
Ink and
watercolour

purpose of work
Daily Newspaper
advertisement

brief
A set of 25
illustrations with a
quirky
interpretation of
corporate facts and
figures. The
sequence involved
a visual countdown
from numbers 1-25

commissioned by
Barry Jennings

company
CKMP

agent
Central Illustration
Agency
36 Wellington
Street
London
WC2E 7BD
t. 020 7240 8925

115 Crystal Palace
Road
East Dulwich
London
SE22 9ES

t. 020 8693 4315
f. 020 8693 4315

ADVERTISING

title
Fire Brigade Hotline

medium
Ink and
watercolour

purpose of work
Daily Newspaper
advertisement

brief
A set of 25
illustrations with a
quirky
interpretation of
corporate facts and
figures. The
sequence involved
a visual countdown
from numbers 1-25

commissioned by
Barry Jennings

company
CKMP

agent
Central Illustration
Agency
36 Wellington
Street
London
WC2E 7BD
t. 020 7240 8925

carolyn gowdy

2c Maynard Close
off Cambria Street
London
SW6 2EN

t. 020 7731 5380
f. 020 7731 5380

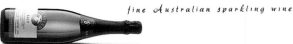

title
Salisbury
Mountaineers Party

medium
Mixed Media

purpose of work
London
Underground
poster
commissioned to
advertise Seaview
sparkling wine
(part of a series)

brief
Seaview, whatever
the do and based
on the notion of
'celebration' for
different affinity
groups who meet
together to drink
wine. These
mountaineers
gather near the
summit of the
stairs

commissioned by
David Dye

company
BMP DDB

michael terry

12 Bartholomew Street
Hythe
Kent
CT21 5BS
t. 01303 269456
f. 01303 269456
email. michael.terry@email-me.co.uk

title
Cave Girl
medium
Gouache
purpose of work
Poster
brief
To illustrate 'Early
Essex girl loves
Martin Day's
breakfast show'
commissioned by
Roger Green
company
Baily-Green-Salter

title
Romeo
medium
Gouache
purpose of work
Poster
brief
To illustrate a
rejected Romeo
character

commissioned by
John Kane
company
Javelin Young &
Rubicam (Dublin)

judges **Tracy Hirst** / Children's Art Director / Transworld

Tim Rose / Senior Designer / Scholastic Children's Books

John Lord / Prinicipal Lecturer / University of Brighton

Sara Fanelli / Illustrator

Illustration by Nelly Dimitranova +44 (0)20 7284 2334

children's books

Children's books

Section winner: Alison Jay

Design process by Derek Brazell

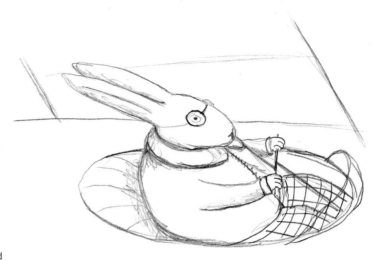

As Alison Jay's red aeroplane sails over it's glowing cliff top landscape, piloted by a bespectacled white rabbit, it's easy to see why Mike Jolley of Templar Publishing chose her for his *Picture This* children's book. 'I wanted a slightly nostalgic Enid Blyton, 1940's feel,' he says, 'and her artwork crosses borders; I like it, my mother would like it, American customers will go for it because it has an American naïve art feel to it, but it's also very English – it'll appeal to a lot of people.'

Samples of Alison's work had been pinned to Mike's wall for some time just waiting for the perfect project. So when the concept of a one word per page picture book was proposed by the company, Alison was the right choice. 'Basically,' says Mike, 'it's a child's first picture book, so each image has to stand on it's own; but then also have all these incidental linking elements which take you through the four seasons.' Mike and editor Dugald Steer wanted images with quite a few layers, so that a parent and child could find and discuss the various elements within the picture. So the rabbit will be featured in his plane, and then appear in the children's bedroom in a minor role.

Once this was worked out Mike went to meet Alison, 'I think it's a really good idea to meet face to face,' he says; and then it was over to her. The initial problems of working out the interlinking images

('I had to draw out a huge map', says Alison), gave way to a smooth ride with the visuals. 'I do tend to like working in my own way,' she adds, 'but because Mike and I were on the same wavelength it worked really well.' Mike required hardly any changes from the pencil roughs that Alison delivered, relying on her to fill in more detail on the coloured artwork.

The freshness of Alison's illustrations make *Picture This* a delightful series of pictures, with the warm colours and playful images surely having fascinated many a child since it's publication in late 1999. It certainly shows that Alison enjoyed this project. 'It's probably the nicest job I've done yet in children's books,' she says from the drawing board of her sixth picture book.

So with both client and illustrator very happy with the final product, would Mike like to work with Alison in the future? 'Absolutely,' he enthuses, 'It's a question of finding a project specifically for her, as soon as she's free. . . I believe she's chokka for the next six months!'

★ winner in childrens' book section
★ winner: *Transworld Children's Book Award*

TRANSWORLD PUBLISHERS LTD

alison jay

14 Ingersoll Road
London
W12 7BD

t. 020 8749 2264

title
1 Aeroplane
2 Bed 3 Dog

medium
Alkyd and varnish
on paper

purpose of work
Children's picture
book

brief
To illustrate a
single word per
page on spread -
each word relates
to the next in some
way

commissioned by
Mike Jolley

company
Templar

agent
The Organisation
69 Caledonian
Road
London
N1 9BT
t. 020 7833 8268

deborah allwright

5 Torrens Street
London
EC1V 1NQ

t. 020 7713 5773
email. DAllwright@cheekymonkey.org.uk

title
Grunter's Birthday

medium
Mixed media

purpose of work
Children's picture
book

brief
Create "Grunter a
pig with attitude"

commissioned by
Mike Jolley

company
The Templar
Company Plc.

agent
Kathy Jakeman
Richmond Business
Centre
23-24 George
Street
Richmond
Surrey
TW9 IVY
t. 017071 225 114

derek brazell

28 Hatton House
Hindmarsh Close
London
E1 8JH

t. 020 7265 1896
f. 020 7265 1896

title
Lima's Red Hot
Chilli

medium
Pencil, crayon and
gouache

purpose of work
Book jacket

brief
To depict the
moment when Lima
eats the amazingly
hot chilli

commissioned by
Mishti Chatterji

company
Mantra Publishing

agent
Artist Partners
14-18 Ham Yard
Great Windmill
Street
London
W1V 8DE
t. 020 7734 7991

john butler

26 Court Road
Tunbridge Wells
Kent
TN4 8ED

t. 01892 521061
f. 01892 514309
m. 07714 347729
email. john.butler7@virgin.net

34
GB

title
Four Wide-eyed
Owls / Tiger
Hunting / Three
Bears

medium
Acrylic and
coloured pencil

purpose of work
Spreads from
children's book

brief
Self-written
children's book

commissioned by
Rosemary Davies

company
Orchard Books

frances cony

21 Tyndalls Park Road
Clifton
Bristol
BS8 1PQ

t. 0117 973 0022
f. 0117 973 0022

title
Slimy Frogs and
Toads

medium
Pen & ink with
coloured pencils

purpose of work
Illustration for
"Spooky Sparklers:
Gordon's Moment
of Glory" by Kath
Mellentin & Tim
Wood

brief
To illustrate the
animal and spectral
residents of an old
house trying to rid
their home of
human incomers

commissioned by
Kate Rhodes

company
Oyster Books

title
What's That
Outside?

medium
Pen & ink with
coloured pencils

purpose of work
Illustration for
"Spooky Sparklers:
Gordon's Moment
of Glory" by Kath
Mellentin & Tim
Wood

brief
The "snotty and
objectionable"
family under attack
by things unknown

commissioned by
Kate Rhodes

company
Oyster Books

frances cony

21 Tyndalls Park Road
Clifton
Bristol
BS8 1PQ

t. 0117 973 0022
f. 0117 973 0022

36
GB

title
Old MacDonald had
a Farm

medium
Pen & ink with
watercolour

purpose of work
Book cover for a
version of the
traditional song
paper-engineered
by Iain Smyth

brief
To illustrate Old
MacDonald and his
chugging tractor,
plus examples of
all the noisy
animals in the
book, leaving
space for title,
authors' names and
animal sounds

commissioned by
Jemima Lumley /
Mandy Suhr

company
Orchard Books

frances cony

21 Tyndalls Park Road
Clifton
Bristol
BS8 1PQ

t. 0117 973 0022
f. 0117 973 0022

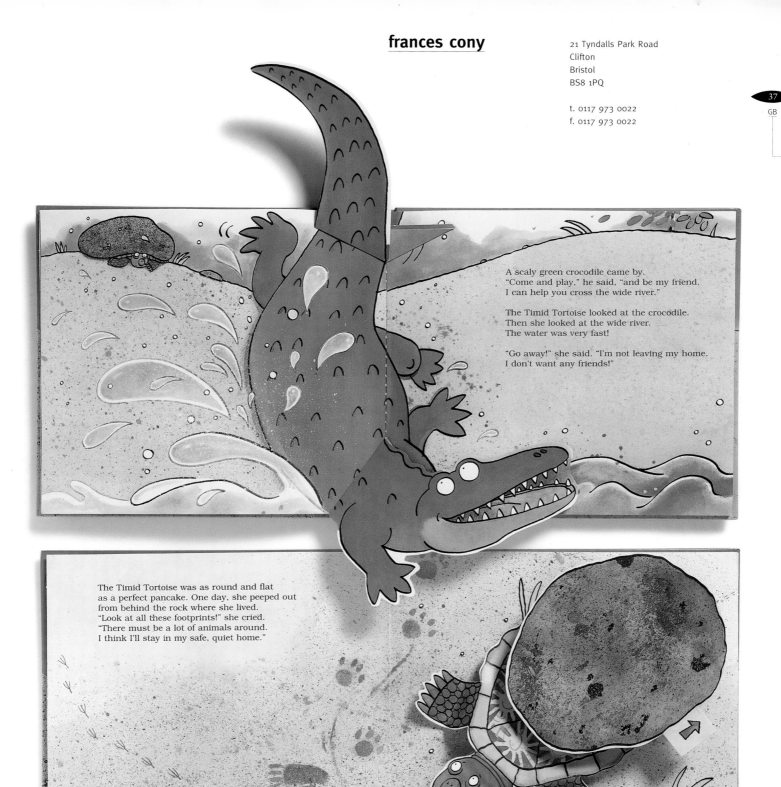

A scaly green crocodile came by.
"Come and play," he said, "and be my friend.
I can help you cross the wide river."

The Timid Tortoise looked at the crocodile.
Then she looked at the wide river.
The water was very fast!

"Go away!" she said. "I'm not leaving my home.
I don't want any friends!"

The Timid Tortoise was as round and flat
as a perfect pancake. One day, she peeped out
from behind the rock where she lived.
"Look at all these footprints!" she cried.
"There must be a lot of animals around.
I think I'll stay in my safe, quiet home."

title
The Timid Tortoise
medium
Pen & ink with
watercolour
purpose of work
Inside and cover
illustrations for the
children's pop-up
book "The Timid
Tortoise" by Linda
Jane Cornwell

brief
To illustrate the
attempts of various
animals to befriend
a shy pancake
tortoise,
incorporating the
paper-engineered
features designed
by Mat Johnstone
commissioned by
Sheri Safran
company
Tango Books

ted dewan

38 Southwood Avenue
London
N6 5RZ

t. 020 8342 8137
f. 020 8347 5321
www.wormworks.com

title
Rumpelstiltskin

medium
Biro, watercolour
and gouache

purpose of work
Book Jacket

brief
Open brief -
illustrate the story
of Rumpelstiltskin
for Magic Bean
series of fairy tales

commissioned by
David Fickling

company
Scholastic

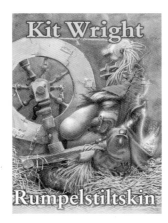

elena gomez

Stonelands
Portsmouth Road
Milford, Godalming
Surrey, GU8 5DR

t 01483 423876
t. 01483 426607
f. 01483 423935

title
The Oxen
medium
Acrylic
purpose of work
Interior illustration
for "Celebrating
Christmas"
children's book

brief
To illustrate the
poem "The Oxen"
using children
carrying lanterns at
night, across a
frosty field towards
a barn
commissioned by
Lois Rock
company
Lion Publishing Plc

title
Christmas Festivity
medium
Acrylic
purpose of work
Promotional poster
for Lion
Publishing's
seasonal books
(also used as a
book jacket and
interior illustration
for "Celebrating
Christmas"
children's book)
brief
To illustrate the
poem "Christmas
Festivity" using
angels decorating a
tree
commissioned by
Lois Rock
company
Lion Publishing Plc

andy hammond

Benington House
93 Aylesbury Road
Wendover
Bucks
HP22 6JN

t. 01296 624439
f. 01296 696198
email.   andyhammond@illustrationweb.com

title
Alfie's Adventures
with: The Romans,
The Anglo Saxons,
The Tudors, The
Vikings, The
Victorians

medium
Pen and ink with
watercolour

purpose of work
Series of children's
books

brief
To create a
character Alfie for a
new series of
children's history
stories. "Fun to
learn" collection

commissioned by
Emma Percival

company
Brilliant Books

agent
Illustration
1 Vicarage Crescent
Clapham
London
SW11 3LP
t. 020 7228 8882

joy gosney

7 Netherfield Road
Finchley
London
N12 8DP
t. 020 8922 7800
m. 0421 622 652

title
Naughty Parents

medium
Oil pastel, gouache, pencil

purpose of work
Bloomsbury children's book

brief
"Oh stop!" shouted a man. "I'm soaked!"

commissioned by
Sarah Odedina

company
Bloomsbury

title
Naughty Parents

medium
Oil pastel, gouache, pencil

purpose of work
Bloomsbury children's book

brief
"Oh dear!" giggled a woman. "Your lollipops are melting"

commissioned by
Sarah Odedina

company
Bloomsbury

title
Naughty Parents

medium
Oil pastel, gouache, pencil

purpose of work
Bloomsbury children's book

brief
"Ah Yes!" said the Lady. "I have two very dirty, wet and sticky parents here who fit that description. They must belong to you!"

commissioned by
Sarah Odedina

company
Bloomsbury

lisa kopper

1 Peary Place
London
E2 0QW

t. 020 8981 4824
f. 020 8981 5609
email.
lisak@dircon.co.uk

title
Daisy Knows Best
(6 slides)

medium
Watercolour, pencil,
ink

purpose of work
Third title in the
'DAISY' series

brief
Clear illustrations
that partly carry the
narrative for the
under fives

commissioned by
Penny Morris

company
Penguin Books

agent
Lisa Eveleigh
Agency
26a Rochester
Square
London
NW1 9SA
t. 020 7267 5245

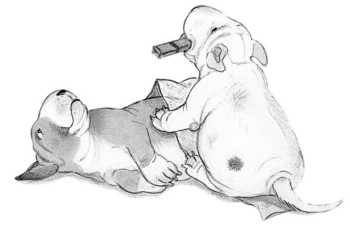

nick hardcastle

98 Eaton road
Norwich
Norfolk
NR4 6PR
t. 01603 452855
f. 01603 452855

title
Howl
medium
Pen and ink
purpose of work
Book illustration -
one in a series
called Vampire and
Werewolf stories
brief
To illustrate a
dramatic scene
from the short
story

commissioned by
Suzanne Carnell
company
Kingfisher
agent
Illustrators.Co
3 Richbourne
Terrace
London
SW8 1AR
t. 020 7793 7000

title
The Werewolf (By
Angela Carter)
medium
Pen and ink
purpose of work
Book illustration -
one in a series
called Vampire and
Werewolf stories
brief
To illustrate a
dramatic and
atmospheric scene
from the short
story
commissioned by
Suzanne Carnell
company
Kingfisher
agent
Illustrators.Co
3 Richbourne
Terrace
London
SW8 1AR
t. 020 7793 7000

title
The Little Mystery
medium
Pen and ink
purpose of work
One in a series
entitled Detective
Stories
brief
To illustrate a
dramatic moment
in the story with
also a sense of
atmosphere
commissioned by
Suzanne Carnell
company
Kingfisher
agent
Illustrators.Co
3 Richbourne
Terrace
London
SW8 1AR
t. 020 7793 7000

title
Cold Money
medium
Pen and ink
purpose of work
One in a series
entitled Detective
Stories
brief
To illustrate a
dramatic and
moody scene from
the story
commissioned by
Suzanne Carnell
company
Kingfisher
agent
Illustrators.Co
3 Richbourne
Terrace
London
SW8 1AR
t. 020 7793 7000

satoshi kambayashi

Flat 2
40 Tisbury Road
Hove
East Sussex
BN3 3BA

t. 01273 771539
f. 01273 771539
email. satoshi.k@virgin.net

title
Molly and the
Snorgle Fly
medium
Line and wash
purpose of work
Children's picture
book

brief
To write and
illustrate a
children's picture
book
commissioned by
Amelia Hoare
company
Brilliant Books

satoshi kambayashi

Flat 2
40 Tisbury Road
Hove
East Sussex
BN3 3BA

t. 01273 771539
f. 01273 771539
email. satoshi.k@virgin.net

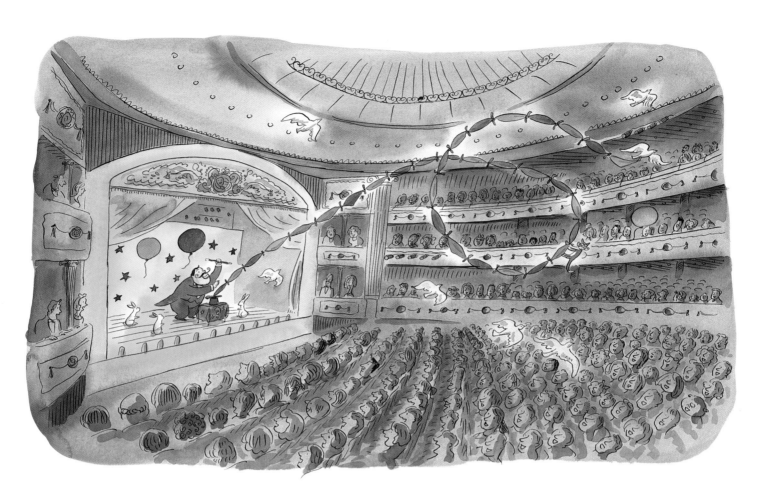

title
The Magic Hat
medium
Line and wash

purpose of work
Children's picture
book

brief
To write and
illustrate a
children's picture
book

commissioned by
Alasdair McWhirter

company
Brilliant Books

richard pargeter

124 Stamford Road
Amblecote
Brierley Hill
West Midlands
DY5 2PZ
t. 01384 832924
f. 01384 832924
email. rparg@globalnet.co.uk

title
"Slurp! Gran Said"

medium
Mixed Media

purpose of work
Illustrated page for children's book 'Runaway Gran' written and illustrated by the artist

brief
Self promotional work. To write and design a humorous gift book for children. Aiming at 8 - 10 year olds using a colourful and mixed media approach

karin littlewood

Courtyard Studio
38 Mount Pleasant
London
WC1X 0AP

t. 020 7833 4113
f. 020 7833 3064

title
Billy's Sunflower

commissioned by
Penny Morris

medium
Watercolour,
gouache

company
"Little Hippo" /
Scholastic

purpose of work
To illustrate the
text "Billy's
Sunflower",
children's book
illustration

agent
Illustrators Co.
3 Richbourne
Terrace
London
SW8 1AR
t. 020 7793 7000

brief
My interpretation
of a simple story of
the relationship
between a boy and
his sunflower
through the
seasons

patrick macallister

23 Vicars Oak Road
London
SE19 1HE

t. 020 8761 5578
f. 020 8761 5578

48

GB

title
Number Crunch

medium
Ink, photoshop

purpose of work
Book jacket design
(two colour print)

brief
Originally titled
"Number
Challenges", six
landscape sketches
were required of
which three would
be chosen to make
up the design

commissioned by
Shelia Ebbutt

company
BEAM

lydia monks

64 Frankfurt Road
Herne Hill
London
SE24 9NY
t. 020 7274 4158
m. 07971 052 529

title
I Wish I Were a
Dog

medium
Mixed Media

purpose of work
Children's book

brief
To illustrate my
own story of a cat
that wishes it were
a dog

commissioned by
Egmont Children's
Books

agent
The Agency
24 Pottery Lane
Holland Park
London
W11 4LZ
t. 020 7727 1346

chris mould

Grove House Farm
Wyke Lane
Oakenshaw
Bradford
West Yorkshire
BD12 7EE

t. 01274 678753
f. 01274 678753
m. 07977 360502

title
Sweeney Todd
Horner (from "A
Haunting We Will
Go")

medium
Black ink, white
emulsion

purpose of work
To illustrate the
poem 'Sweeney
Todd Horner'

brief
To illustrate, with
humour, the given
poem, whilst
retaining the
ghostly theme of
the book

commissioned by
Marilyn Watts

company
Oxford University
Press

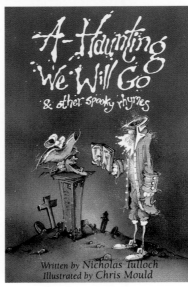

title
The Ghost's Arrival

medium
Black ink, white
emulsion

purpose of work
To produce an
opening endpaper
for the book "A
Haunting We Will
Go"

brief
To provide an
image which
represents the
beginning of the
book

commissioned by
Marilyn Watts

company
Oxford University
Press

title
Laughing His Head
Off (from "A
Haunting We Will
Go")

medium
Coloured inks,
some acrylic

purpose of work
To provide a colour
cover for the title
"A Haunting We
Will Go"

brief
To produce an
image to represent
and give a feel for
the 'Horror with
Humour' theme of
the work

commissioned by
Marilyn Watts

company
Oxford University
Press

bee willey

7 Atlas Mews
London
E8 2NE

t. 020 7254 8874
t. 020 8986 5933
f. 020 7254 8874
email. bee.willey@virgin.net
www.illustration-uk.com

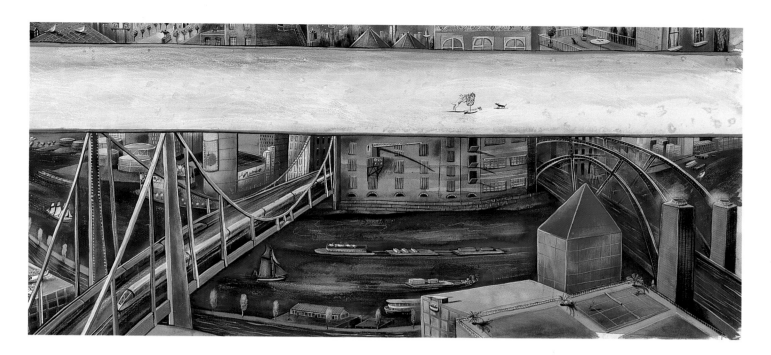

title	commissioned by	title	commissioned by
River Story	Louise Jackson	River Story	Louise Jackson
medium	**company**	**medium**	**company**
Mixed Media	Walker Books	Mixed Media	Walker Books
purpose of work	**agent**	**purpose of work**	**agent**
To illustrate the	Illustration	To illustrate the	Illustration
path of the river	1 Vicarage Crescent	path of the river	1 Vicarage Crescent
from source to sea,	London	from source to sea,	London
crossing the	SW11 3LP	crossing the	SW11 3LP
various landscapes,	t. 020 7228 8882	various landscapes,	t. 020 7228 8882
(erosion, city		(erosion, city	
scapes, fauna and		scapes, fauna and	
floral relevant to		floral relevant to	
each location)		each location)	
brief		**brief**	
Through the city		Through the plains	

michael terry

12 Bartholomew Street
Hythe
Kent
CT21 5BS

t. 01303 269456
f. 01303 269456
email. michael.terry@email-me.co.uk

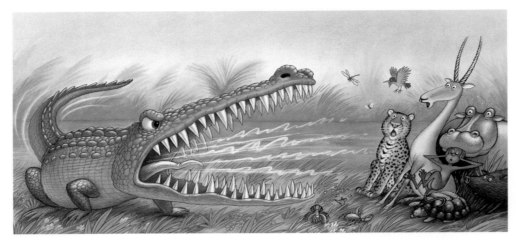

title
The Selfish
Crocodile

medium
Gouache, pen &
ink, colour pencil

purpose of work
Children's picture
book

brief
To illustrate a story
about a selfish
crocodile and his
relationship with
the other animals

commissioned by
Emma Matthewson

company
Bloomsbury

michael terry

12 Bartholomew Street
Hythe
Kent
CT21 5BS
t. 01303 269456
f. 01303 269456
email. michael.terry@email-me.co.uk

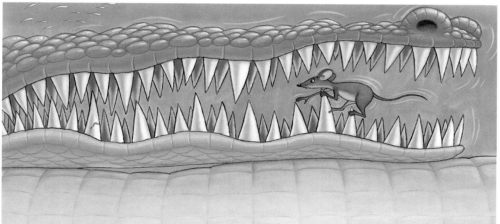

title
The Selfish
Crocodile

medium
Gouache, pen &
ink, colour pencil

purpose of work
Children's picture
book

brief
To illustrate a story
about a selfish
crocodile and his
relationship with
the other animals

commissioned by
Emma Matthewson

company
Bloomsbury

title
Masha And The
Firebird

medium
Printing inks and
collaged papers

purpose of work
Children's book
illustration

brief
Provide
illustrations for
'Masha and The
Firebird' including
cover and all inside
illustrations

commissioned by
Illustration

agent
Illustration
1 Vicarage Crescent
London
SW11 3LP
t. 020 7228 8882

judges   **Matilda Harrison** / Illustrator

Gordon Beckett / Design Editor / Sunday Times

Sian Lewis / Art Director / Saturday Express Magazine

Illustration by Adam Graff +44 (0)20 8521 7182

editorial

Editorial

Section winner: James Marsh Food Fight

Design process by Stuart Briers

58

GB

Despite the increasing restrictions of recent years the editorial field continues to offer the illustrator the creative space all too often denied them in other areas of the industry. For that reason it is probably here that the truest expression of the illustrator's art can be found.

Successful editorial illustrations encompass a wide range of styles and approaches but the best work results when the artist has married a clear concept with an exactitude of technique. A perfect example of this can be found in *Food Fight* by James Marsh.

James was commissioned by Paul Lussier of Time Magazine (UK) in July 1998 to produce a cover image for a main feature article on genetically engineered food (one of the first such articles to appear before the subsequent flood of media interest in genetically modified products).

Although James was sent the text in full, a more general image was required rather than anything too specific. Some initial ideas were submitted.

'My first ideas revolved around the use of families and lab jars – that sort of imagery which the client felt were a bit too scientific. After a bit of a chat on the phone I came up with the idea of the double helix. The rest just fell into place.'

Tomatoes were the ideal addition because of their link with genetically modified food and also their shape reads clearly as a molecular structure. The inclusion of a small figure lends the image a Jack and the Beanstalk quality ideally suited to the subject matter.

A small pencil sketch (130mm x 100mm) was prepared, as reproduced here, and faxed to the client.

'They loved the concept and gave me the go-ahead with one comment, a useful one, which was to make the tomatoes less rounded/graphic and more natural in shape like the beefsteak tomato.'

The sketch was then further refined and enlarged to A3: 'A comfortable working size that can accommodate the level of detail the picture requires and also practical for scanning purposes.'

As James works intuitively with colour there is no necessity for any further visuals so it's straight on to the painting. Working with acrylics on canvas (hand mounted on board) the background is first painted to a high level of finish before the foreground is traced down and rendered.

'The colouring on this job was pretty straightforward. I knew the colours I wanted would be reds, blues and white that I believe are the colours used on the scientific models of molecular structures. Also, the red edging used by Time would tie in well with the reds of the tomatoes.'

As Time magazine is a weekly publication deadlines are invariably tight.

The initial accepted sketch was faxed on 23rd July and the artwork completed on 24th July.

'This was a smooth job from start to finish', says James, 'and the client loved the illustration.'

★ **editorial section winner**
★ **award winner:** *AOIClient Award*

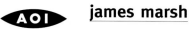

james marsh

21 Elms Road
London
SW4 9ER

t. 020 7622 9530
f. 020 7498 6851

59
GB

title
Food Fight

medium
Acrylics on canvas

purpose of work
Cover for magazine

brief
Open brief to
design cover for
feature about
genetic engineering

commissioned by
Paul Lussier

company
Time Inc

james marsh

21 Elms Road
London
SW4 9ER

t. 020 7622 9530
f. 020 7498 6851

title
Lord of Misrule

medium
Acrylics on canvas

purpose of work
3/4 DPS in
Magazine

brief
Open brief for
portrait of Mugabe
to support damning
article

commissioned by
Martin Collier

company
Readers Digest

title
Congratulations
you're a Father!

medium
Acrylics on textured
paper

purpose of work
Whole page in
magazine

brief
Open brief to
illustrate article
about being
ordained on the
Internet

commissioned by
Lisa Brown

company
YAHOO! Internet
Life

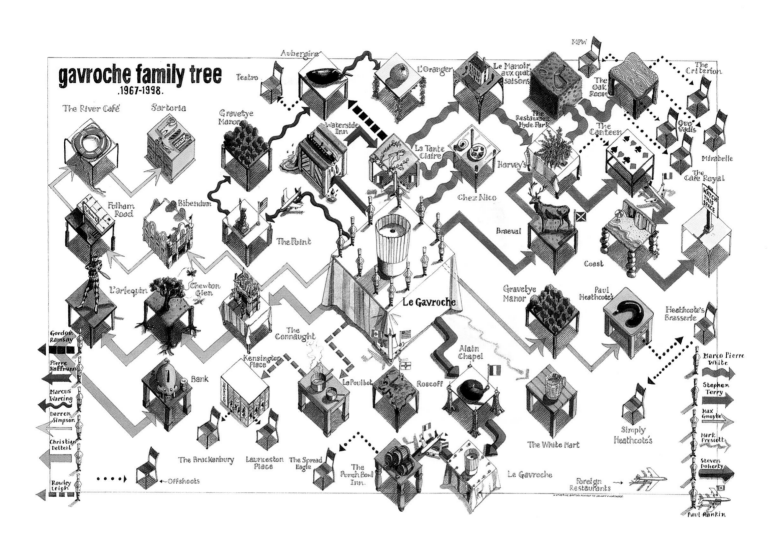

title
Gavroche Family
Tree

medium
Pen and Ink with
watercolour

purpose of work
To show "family
tree" of chefs at
the Gavroche

brief
To illustrate the
"family tree" of
chefs that started
their career at the
Gavroche

commissioned by
Graham Ball

company
Times Magazine

agent
Folio
10 Gate Street
Lincolns in Fields
London
WC2 A3HP
t. 020 7242 9562

See Agent

title
The Market
Capitalisation
Imperative

medium
Chalk Pastels

purpose of work
To illustrate an
article on corporate
strategy in a
globalising world

brief
To illustrate an
article on corporate
strategy in a
globalising world

commissioned by
James Coulson

company
McKinsey & Co.

agent
Illustration
1 Vicarage Crescent
London
SW11 3LP
t. 020 7228 8882

title
Global Psychology

medium
Chalk Pastels

purpose of work
To illustrate an
article for
'community care'
mag

brief
Global Psychology
commissioned by
Stephanie Fenner

company
Community Care
Magazine

agent
Illustration
1 Vicarage Crescent
London
SW11 3LP
t. 020 7228 8882

john bradley

18 Rutland Street
Old Whittington
Chesterfield
Derbyshire
S41 9DJ

t. 01246 238953
f. 01246 238953

EDITORIAL

title
Fashion

medium
Pen and ink

purpose of work
Illustrate on going
series reviewing
various net sites

brief
Provide humourous
interpretation of
'Fashion' for review
of net sites

commissioned by
Anthony Johnston

company
Net Magazine

christopher corr

27 Myddelton Street
London
EC1
t. 020 7833 5699

title
A Different Way to Do...

medium
Gouache

purpose of work
Illustrations for Radio Times holiday supplement

brief
A set of five illustrations showing alternatives to the normal tourist attractions when on holiday in Cuba, India, China, Mexico and the Caribbean

commissioned by
Tracey Gardiner

company
Radio Times

bill sanderson

Fernleigh
Huntingdon Road
Houghton
Cambridgeshire
PE17 2AU

t. 01480 461506
f. 01480 461506

michael sheehy

115 Crystal Palace Road
East Dulwich
London
SE22 9ES

t. 020 8693 4315

title
Nana

medium
Scraper board and inks

purpose of work
Illustration for Radio 4's Book at Bedtime

brief
Zola's depiction of immortality in French society centres on the voluptuous 18 year old Nana, whose titillating theatrical shows cause four men to fall under her spell

commissioned by
Matthew Bookman

company
Radio Times

title
Inside Track

medium
Mixed media

purpose of work
Illustration for Radio 4 documentary

brief
Stinky the pig is a well loved pet, but doesn't realise the fate of hundreds of other pigs who live alongside him at the abattoir!

commissioned by
Tracey Gardiner

company
Radio Times

bill butcher

Sans Works
1 Sans Walk
London
EC1R oLT

t. 020 7336 6642
f. 020 7253 7675

title
The Web in Your
Hand
medium
Acrylic
purpose of work
Cover illustration
for The Guardian
(on line)
brief
To illustrate The
Web in Your Hand

commissioned by
Vick Keegan
company
The Guardian

stuart briers

186 Ribblesdale Road
London
SW16 6QY

t. 020 8677 6203
f. 020 8677 6203
email. stuart.briers@btinternet.com

title
Widows Estate

medium
Digital

purpose of work
To illustrate article

brief
To accompany
article about how
ones estate can
be pilfered unless
proper provision is
made

commissioned by
Anton Klusener

company
Forbes Magazine

title
A Different Vision

medium
Digital

purpose of work
To accompany
article

brief
To depict a new
way for companies
to look at their
changing
technological needs

commissioned by
Mary Workman

company
Custom
Communications

MAGNET
ARTISTS

nick dewar

564 First Avenue
APT. 12-S
New York
NY 10016
USA

t. 001 212 686 1376
f. 001 212 686 1376

title
Senses and
Sensibility

medium
Acrylic

purpose of work
Editorial

brief
To illustrate the
phenomena of
Synaesthesia, the
ability to hear
colours, see
sounds and taste
music

commissioned by
Etienne Gilfillan

company
Fortean Times

agent
UK
Eastwing
98 Columbia Road
London
E2 7QB
t. 020 7613 5580
USA
Kate Larkworthy
80 Nassau Street
#202
New York
NY 10038
t. 001 212 964 9141

cyrus deboo

57 Ormonde Court
Upper Richmond Road
London
SW15 6TP

t. 020 8788 8167
f. 020 8788 8167
m. 07050 039 477
e-mail. cyrus.deboo@virgin.net

title
Road Rage

medium
Digital

purpose of work
Editorial Illustration

brief
To illustrate high
pollution levels
inside cars could
be causing road
rage

commissioned by
Steve Anyiwo

company
You Magazine

title
Drink Drive?

medium
Digital

purpose of work
Editorial Illustration

brief
Your dinner guest
is drunk. Try to
convince him or her
that they shouldn't
attempt to drive
themselves home

commissioned by
Gary Locherby

company
You Magazine

philip disley

34 East Wapping Quay
Liverpool
L3 4BU

t. 0151 709 9126
f. 0151 709 9126
m. 0973 298992

title
Heading for
Disaster

medium
Gouache and ink

purpose of work
1/4 page illustration

brief
To decorate an
article about how
the Bordelais are
ignorant of
dropping sales

commissioned by
Peter Bairstow /
Linda Burrows

company
*Sunday Times,
Style Magazine*

Agent
Harriet Kastaris
3301A South
Jefferson Avenue
St Louis
Missouri 63118
USA
t. 001 314 773
2600
(American
Commissions only)

jovan djordjevic

9 Fairlop Road
Leytonstone
London
E11 1BL
t. 020 8539 3892
f. 020 8539 3893
email. jovan@jovan.demon.co.uk

title
Net Closes on the
Mortgage Sharks

medium
Photocopy,
watercolour, pen,
ink & digital

purpose of work
Illustrate finance
article

commissioned by
Miles Dickson

company
Sunday Telegraph

title
Microsoft Office
2000 - Office
Towers

medium
Photodye,
photocopy, pen,
ink & digital

purpose of work
Illustrate
introduction of
Office 2000

commissioned by
Alex Westthorp

company
Dennis Publishing

client
Computer Shopper

emma dodd

4 Northington Street
London
WC1N 2JT

t. 020 7430 9146
f. 020 7430 9156
email. emma@blackhat.demon.co.uk

72
GB

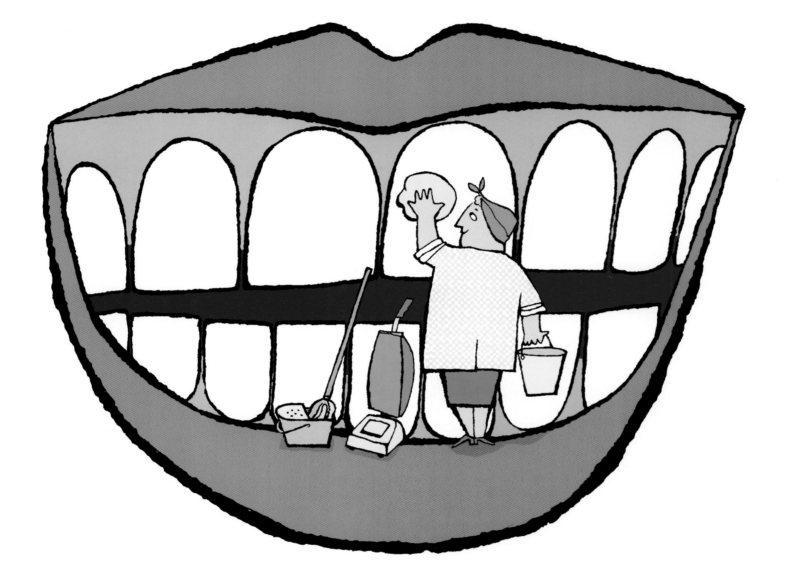

title
Dental Hygiene
medium
Photoshop
purpose of work
Illustrate health
page in Sunday
supplement
brief
Illustrate article on
dental hygiene

commissioned by
Jonathan Bulstrode-
Whitelocke
company
The Sunday
Express Magazine
agent
Black Hat Ltd.
4 Northington
Street
London
WC1N 2JG
t. 020 7430 9146

carl flint

520 Clerkenwell Workshops
31 Clerkenwell Close
London
EC1R 0AT

t. 020 7336 8989
f. 020 7336 8989
pager. 07669 048881

title
See No Evil, Read No Evil

medium
Photocopy, collage and ink

purpose of work
To illustrate an article on "Freedom of Information Act"

brief
To show that it is easy to find out what Blair had for breakfast but not details of weapons sales under new act

commissioned by
Marc Pechart

company
The Big Issue

geoff grandfield

30 Allen Road
London
N16 8SA

t. 020 7241 1523
f. 020 7241 1523
m. 0831 534 192

title
Sham Rock

medium
Chalk Pastel

purpose of work
Article for G2
Section of The
Guardian

brief
Are record co-
executives carving
up the industry to
get to No.1?

commissioned by
The Guardian

geoff grandfield

30 Allen Road
London
N16 8SA

t. 020 7241 1523
f. 020 7241 1523
m. 0831 534 192

title
We're off on a
learning marathon
medium
Chalk Pastel
purpose of work
Article for Online
section of T.E.S.
brief
Illustrate the new
national grid for
learning
commissioned by
Times Supplement

geoff grandfield

30 Allen Road
London
N16 8SA

t. 020 7241 1523
f. 020 7241 1523
m. 0831 534 192

title
I Do, Do you

medium
Chalk Pastel

purpose of work
Article for G2
Section of the
Guardian

brief
Can open
marriages ever
work?

commissioned by
The Guardian

jon d hamilton

1 Bickley Road
London
E10 7AQ

t. 020 8556 3757
f. 020 8926 3029
pager. 01523 446 401
email. jon@jondhamilton.demon.co.uk

EDITORIAL

title
Extensions

medium
Toy dolls, paint,
balsa, digital
camera, photshop
5.02

purpose of work
Illustration for BBC
Good Homes
Magazine

brief
To accompany
article on how to
make your house
grow with your
family

commissioned by
Helen Benfield

company
BBC Good Homes

andrew foster

150 Curtain Road
Back Building
1st Floor Studio
London
EC2A 3AT

t. 0966 283 237
f. 020 7613 0731

78
GB

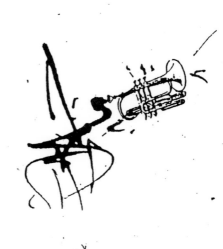

title
Musical Individuals

medium
Ink, collage and
pencil

purpose of work
9 spot headings for
London
Philharmonic
Orchestra
1999/2000
(yearbook,
magazine)

brief
Communicate the
energy and
excitement of the
individuals within
the LPO

chuan khoo

27 Whitmore Street
Maidstone
Kent
ME16 8JX

t. 01622 721 987
f. 01622 721 987

title
Tailor Made

medium
Acrylic

purpose of work
Editorial illustration

brief
Small Self
Administered
Schemes (SSAS's) a
type of company
pension scheme
which can allow
directors of small
companies to tailor
make a pension
fund

commissioned by
Sarah Henney

company
Bloomberg Money

claire harper

Pikes Cottage
Sandy Lane
Brampford Speke
Exeter
EX5 5HW
t. 01392 841967
f. 01392 841936
pager. 04325 269358

title
Angel on a bicycle

medium
Gouache

purpose of work
Personal project

brief
Experimental line
drawing

title
Musical Bird

medium
Indian ink

purpose of work
Personal project

brief
Experimental
drawing around
musical symbols

title
Facilities
Management

medium
Metal

purpose of work
Black and White
cover of "Forty
Magazine"

brief
Even companies
that make their
running seem
effortless need the
support of a well
oiled machine

commissioned by
Stephen Quirke

company
Atom Publishing

agent
The Inkshed
98 Columbia Road
London
E2 7QB
t. 020 7613 2323

robin heighway-bury

1st Floor Studio
Back Building
150 Curtain Road
London
EC2A 3AR

t. 020 7739 0005
f. 020 7613 0731

title
Roughage

medium
Ink, collage,
photocopy &
acrylic

purpose of work
To illustrate food
article

brief
To illustrate an
article comparing
various high fibre
cereals

commissioned by
Andie Pemberton

company
BBC Good Food
Magazine

agent
Thorogood
Illustration
5 Dryden Street
London
WC2E 9NW
t. 020 7829 8468

clare yull mackie

21A Ursula Street
London
SW11 3DW

t 020 7223 8649
f. 020 7223 4119

title
The Great Squirrel Turnaround

medium
Watercolour and ink

purpose of work
To illustrate regular column "Tales from the Urban Jungle"

brief
A humorous illustration to show that squirrels become thugs when living in the city

commissioned by
Sian Lewis, Angela Lamb

company
Saturday Express Magazine

agent
Eileen McManhon & Co.
P.O. Box 1062
Bayonne
NY 07002
USA
t. 001 201 436 436

paul slater

22 Partridge Close
Chesham
Bucks
HP5 3LH

t 01494 786 780
t. 01494 792 562
f. 01494 792 562

title
San Lorenzo

medium
Acrylic

purpose of work
To illustrate regular 'literary lunch' page

brief
To illustrate a meal in a restaurant set in the seventies with louche, B list characters written up in a book review

commissioned by
Sian Lewis, Christine Sullivan

company
Saturday Express Magazine

agent
Thorogood Illustration
5 Dryden Street
London
WC2E 9NW
t.020 7829 8468

spike gerrell

Basement Flat
1c Oakfield Road
London
N4 4NH

t 020 7272 6926
f. 020 7272 6926

title
Footballs Coming Home

medium
Acrylic on paper

purpose of work
To illustrate an article on football

brief
To illustrate in a humorous way, the requirements needed to become a football couch potato

commissioned by
Sian Lewis, Joe Wilkes

company
Saturday Express Magazine

satoshi kambayashi

Flat 2
40 Tisbury Road
Hove
East Sussex
BN3 3BA

t. 01273 771539
f. 01273 771539
email. satoshi.k@virgin.net

title
Horrors of
Passengers Without
Etiquettes

medium
Line and wash

purpose of work
Editorial

brief
To illustrate the
problem caused by
lack of on-board
etiquette on
aeroplanes

commissioned by
William Higgins

company
First Class

title
Boiler

medium
Line and wash

purpose of work
Editorial

brief
To illustrate an
amusing
mechanism for a
boiler

commissioned by
Amy Swanson

company
Good
Housekeeping

satoshi kambayashi

Flat 2
40 Tisbury Road
Hove
East Sussex
BN3 3BA

t. 01273 771539
f. 01273 771539
email. satoshi.k@virgin.net

title
Soothing Effect

medium
Line and wash

purpose of work
Editorial

brief
To illustrate the
effect of music on
children who have
a problem
concentrating on
work

commissioned by
Maxine Chung

company
TES

agent
Ian Flemming &
Associates
t. 020 7734 8701

title
Growing Wine List

medium
Line and wash

purpose of work
Editorial

brief
To illustrate the
situation where
wine lists at
restaurants are
getting too large

commissioned by
Angela Dukes

company
Food & Travel

title
Mad Biro-Man

medium
Line and wash

purpose of work
Editorial

brief
To illustrate an
article about office
people: Mad biro-
man who uses
multi-coloured ball-
point pen

commissioned by
Mark Porter

company
The Guardian

peter knock

17 Nelson Drive
Leigh-on-Sea
Essex
SS9 1DA

t. 01702 476885
f. 01702 476885
pager. 0336 750 115

title
Summertime in a
Human
medium
Watercolour
purpose of work
Magazine
illustration
brief
General advice on
preventing catching
a winter cold, and
the avoidance of
touch as a
deterrent

commissioned by
Martin Colyer
company
Readers Digest
Magazine

henning löhlein

Bristol Craft & Design Centre
6 Leonard Lane
Bristol
BS1 1EA

t. 0117 929 9077
f. 0117 929 9077
m. 07711 285202

title
Bull with Vertigo

medium
Acrylic

purpose of work
Cover illustration

brief
To paint a bull that
has vertigo. The
US stock market
was having a bull
run

title
Ward Leaders
medium
3D mixed media
purpose of work
Front cover of
Nursing Times
brief
Article about how
nurses are being
groomed and
nurtured

agent
Private View
9 North Cross Road
East Dulwich
London
SE22 9ET
t. 020 8299 1392
f. 020 8299 4627

glen mcbeth

No.12
37 Sandport Street
Edinburgh
EH6 6EP

t. 0131 555 0576
f. 0131 555 0576
m. 0771 359 0498

89
GB

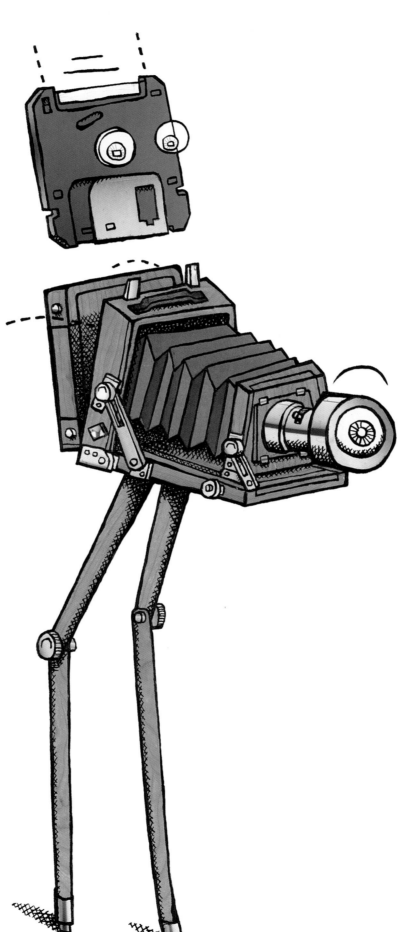

title
Digital Camera
medium
Pen, ink and
collage
purpose of work
Magazine
illustration

brief
To illustrate the
advances in
photography
commissioned by
Computer Easy
(Germany)

mark mcclure

40 Davis Road
Acton
London
W3 7SG

t. 020 8354 1111
pager. 07654 325 233
email. mark.mcc@virgin.net

90
GB

title
Neutrinos
medium
Mixed and Mac
purpose of work
Editorial spread
illustration

brief
Illustrate article on
"Neutrinos"
particles being
observed in Japan -
as they strike water
particles and emit
light. Particles
morph between 3
states of different
mass

commissioned by
David Knight
company
New Scientist
magazine

paul powis

Four Seasons
Battenhall Avenue
Worcester
WR5 2HW

t. 01905 357 563
f. 01905 357 563

title
The Golden Valley

medium
Acrylic

purpose of work
Magazine
Illustration

brief
Demonstration of
landscape painting
using liquitex paint

commissioned by
Neil Montgomery

company
Liquitex

shane mcgowan

23a Parkholme Road
London
E8 3AG

t. 020 7249 6444
f. 020 7249 6444
email. shane.mcgowan@virgin.net

title	**commissioned by**
Prosperity For Now	Paul Lussiere
medium	**company**
Gouache and ink	Time Magazine
purpose of work	**agent**
To illustrate article	The Organisation
for Finance	69 Caledonian
brief	Road
Short term	London
optimism, long	N1 9BT
term anxiety	t. 020 7833 8268
predicted by	
economists for	
global growth.	
Capture that simply	

belle mellor

Flat 3
12 Lansdowne
Street
Hove
East Sussex
BN3 1FQ

t. 01273 732604
f. 01273 732604
m. 0973 463 942

title
Red Nosed Wine
Tasters

medium
Pen and ink

purpose of work
Editorial

brief
Wine tasting event
for Comic Relief

commissioned by
Dominic Ray

company
Comic Relief

agent
Three in a Box Inc
468 Queen Street
East
#104 Box 03
Toronto on Msaitt
Canada
t. 001 416 367 2446

title
The Lure of the
Trumpet

medium
Pen and ink

purpose of work
Editorial

brief
To illustrate a
quote on the Evil
influence of
contemporary
music on young
minds

commissioned by
Simon Moriss

company
BBC Music
Magazine

agent
Three in a Box Inc
468 Queen Street
East
#104 Box 03
Toronto on Msaitt
Canada
t. 001 416 367 2446

belle mellor

Flat 3
12 Lansdowne Street
Hove
East Sussex
BN3 1FQ

t. 01273 732604
f. 01273 732604
m. 0973 463 942

title
Live Music

medium
Pen and ink

purpose of work
Editorial

brief
To illustrate the
benefits of listening
to live music

commissioned by
Simon Moriss

company
BBC Music Magazine

agent
Three in a Box Inc
468 Queen Street
East
#104 Box 03
Toronto on Msaitt
Canada
t. 001 416 367 2446

belle mellor

Flat 3
12 Lansdowne
Street
Hove
East Sussex
BN3 1FQ

t. 01273 732604
f. 01273 732604
m. 0973 463 942

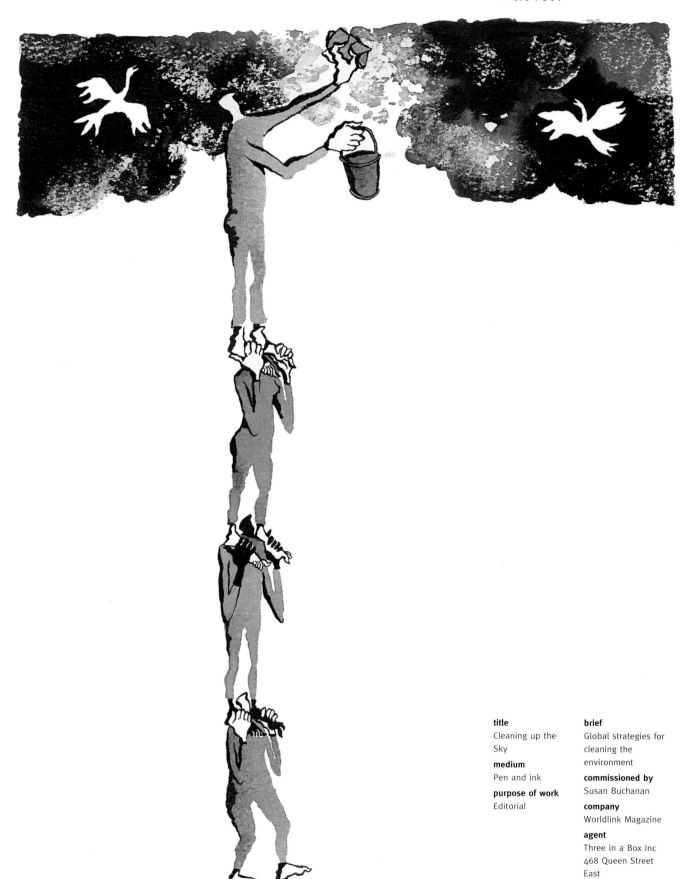

title
Cleaning up the
Sky

medium
Pen and ink

purpose of work
Editorial

brief
Global strategies for
cleaning the
environment

commissioned by
Susan Buchanan

company
Worldlink Magazine

agent
Three in a Box Inc
468 Queen Street
East
#104 Box 03
Toronto on Msaitt
Canada
t. 001 416 367 2446

ali pellatt

First Floor Studio
Back Building
150 Curtain Road
London
EC2A 3AR

t. 020 8772 0332
f. 020 7613 0731
m. 07932 726 725

title
Tony's Cronies
medium
Montage, pastels
purpose of work
Editorial
brief
To show Tony Blair
as the supposed
master of his
political domain
but he is in fact
manipulated by
outside specialist
advisors
commissioned by
Paul Holmes
company
Public Finance
Magazine
agent
Magnet
First Floor Studio
Back Building
150 Curtain Road
London
EC2A 3AR
t. 020 8772 0332

MAGNET
ARTISTS

daniel pudles

8 Herschell Road
London
SE23 1EG

t. 020 8699 8540
f. 020 8699 8540

EDITORIAL

title
Fighting Talk

medium
Print from woodcut

purpose of work
An illustration for
the Guardian's
Women's Section

brief
How men and
women argue
differently

commissioned by
Roger Browning

company
The Guardian

title
Safe as...

medium
Black and white ink
line (and Macintosh
scan)

purpose of work
To illustrate article
about investors'
fear of recession

brief
To illustrate article
about investors'
fear of recession
commissioned by
Andy Jacques

company
Emap / Finance

agent
Illustration
1 Vicarage Crescent
London
SW11 3LP
t. 020 7228 8882

chris robson

13 Whatley Road
Clifton
Bristol
BS8 2PS

t. 0117 973 7694
f. 0117 973 7694
mobile. 0797 137 9354
email. cbrobson@aol.com

title
Data Jockeys

medium
Acrylic

purpose of work
Magazine
illustration

brief
Article about
simultaneous data
and voice
transmissions on
the same phone
lines

commissioned by
Jane Ure Smith

company
Miller Freeman
(New York)

michael sheehy

115 Crystal Palace Road
East Dulwich
London
SE22 9ES

t. 020 8693 4315
f. 020 8693 4315

100

GB

title
The Review Body

medium
Ink and
watercolour

purpose of work
Magazine cover

brief
To express an
employee's feelings
of panic, fear and
lack of control
when faced with a
review of standards
and efficiency

commissioned by
Stephanie Fenner

company
Reed Business
Publishing

agent
Central Illustration
Agency
36 Wellington
Street
London
WC2E 7BD
t. 020 7240 8925

david smith

65 Breech Lane
Walton-on-the-Hill
Surrey
KT20 7SJ

t. 01737 814189
f. 01737 814190
email. dsmith.assoc@virgin.net

101
GB

title
Stealing Beauty

medium
Collage

purpose of work
Front cover
illustration for
Sunday Times
(books section)

brief
Open brief to
illustrate review of
book about
cosmetic surgery
'venus envy'

commissioned by
Denise Beckwith

company
Sunday Times

nancy tolford

20 Park Road
Walthamstow
London
E17 7QF

t. 020 8520 9204
f. 020 8520 9204
email. ntolford@appleonline.net

title
Perfume in Glass

medium
Digital

purpose of work
Review of wines in
the Saturday
Telegraph

commissioned by
John Morris

company
Saturday Telegraph

title
King for a Day

medium
Digital

purpose of work
To illustrate "Self
Critical" a weekly
column written by
Will Self

brief
Article about the
recipient of the
"Dad of the year
Award" presented
on Father's Day

commissioned by
Graham Ball

company
Saturday Times
Magazine

paul wearing

Unit B4
Metropolitan Wharf
Wapping Wall
London
E1 9SS

t. 020 7481 4653
f. 020 7481 4654
email. paulwearing@illustrator.demon.co.uk

title
Food for thought

medium
Digital

purpose of work
To illustrate article
on GM food

brief
To illustrate the
combination of
unnatural genes
and chemicals in
new foods

commissioned by
Tom Shone

company
Room Magazine

judges

Rosemary Sandberg / Agent

Geoff Grandfield / Illustrator

Simon Davis / Art Director / Random House

Fig Taylor / Portfolio Consultant

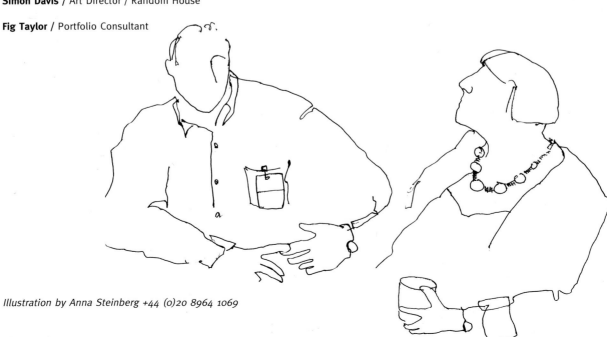

Illustration by Anna Steinberg +44 (0)20 8964 1069

general books

General books

Section winner: Michael Pisarev The Count of Monte Cristo

Design process by Derek Brazell

The deep atmosphere of Roman Pisarev's illustrations for Alexandre Dumas' *The Count of Monte Cristo* draw you into their shadowy intrigues with a maze of fine lines and subtly lit compositions. 'His technique gives a lot of nineteenth century atmosphere, very like fine engravings,' says Joe Whitlock Blundell, Production Director at the Folio Society. Having already illustrated *Classic Russian Short Stories* for Folio, Roman was the ideal choice when they decided to produce *The Count of Monte Cristo*. 'I thought he was brilliant,' continues Joe, 'He has a great sense of the gothic and he does tremendously good research into costumes, horse bridles and all the details you need to do this kind of work.'

Roman, who lives in St Petersburg, but travels to Britain several times a year, confirms this. 'I find all necessary reference materials for the illustrations in books, museums and libraries, both in the UK and Russia. It's not an easy task, but I enjoy it immensely.' His excess luggage bill is witness to the huge amount of purchases from London's art bookshops.

Roman does not resort to models for the detailed characters in his drawings; 'I have twenty years professional education during which I have drawn models in different positions for three to six hours every day so now everything comes from my head.' Joe likes to give illustrators as much freedom as possible and gave Roman his usual open brief of a given number of illustrations spread well throughout the book.

Joe did not request roughs from Roman, 'I trust him, as I do all artists,' and professes himself delighted with the final drawings. Roman's compositions included a split image; a panoramic scene above every illustration, which Joe considered 'a brilliant idea' as the thousand page book is very filmic in

it's scope. 'The originals are amazing,' he continues, 'Roman is fantastically patient, and he's able to put in all these very, very fine lines, How he does it, I don't know!' However, when Roman is quizzed on how he does it, he replies that completing the actual technical drawing does not take a long time, 'The majority of time is taken up with drafts, choice of materials and composition. My hands don't tire as much as my eyes and head!'

They are both thrilled that these illustrations won the General Book section of *Images 24*. Roman, as it was the first time he'd taken part in a British illustration competition and Joe because it confirmed his faith in the power of these pictures. He had predicted in last year's Folio Society members newsletter that these illustrations were going to be regarded as classics, 'So I was delighted to be able to write and say this year that my prediction had come true and was endorsed by the AOI.'

Folio books and the Pisarev style are obviously an ideal partnership. Roman is currently illustrating his third book for the Society, a new translation of *The Legends of King Arthur* and as he says, 'I would always be happy to work for the Folio Society as they have excellent taste in literature.'

roman pisarev

c/o Sarah Powell-Pisareva
PO Box 8
SF-53501 Lappeenranta
Suomi
Finland

107
GB

title
The Count of
Monte Cristo

commission by
Joe Whitlock
Blundell

medium
Ink

company
The Folio Society

purpose of work
One of twenty
illustrations for the
novel

brief
To illustrate
Alexandre Dumas'
The Count of
Monte Cristo

peter gudynas

89 Hazelwell Crescent
Stirchley
Birmingham
B30 2QE

t: 0121 459 0080
f: 0121 459 0080
email: peter@zapart.demon.co.uk

title
Teranesia

medium
Digital

purpose of work
Book Cover

brief
A novel by Greg Egan, concerning cross species genetic engineering and accelerated evolutionary mutation, affecting a certain species of butterfly and how this genetic strain, in turn, effects human beings.

commissioned by
Carl D Galian

client
Harper Collins [USA]

agent
Alan Lynch/Arena Artists
11 Kings Ridge Road
Long Valley
NJ 07852 USA
t. 001 980 813 8718

mick armson

Big Orange
2nd Floor
Back Building
150 Curtain Road
London
EC2A 3AR

t. 020 7739 7765
t. 020 8293 4850
f. 020 7613 2341
m. 0976 575 970

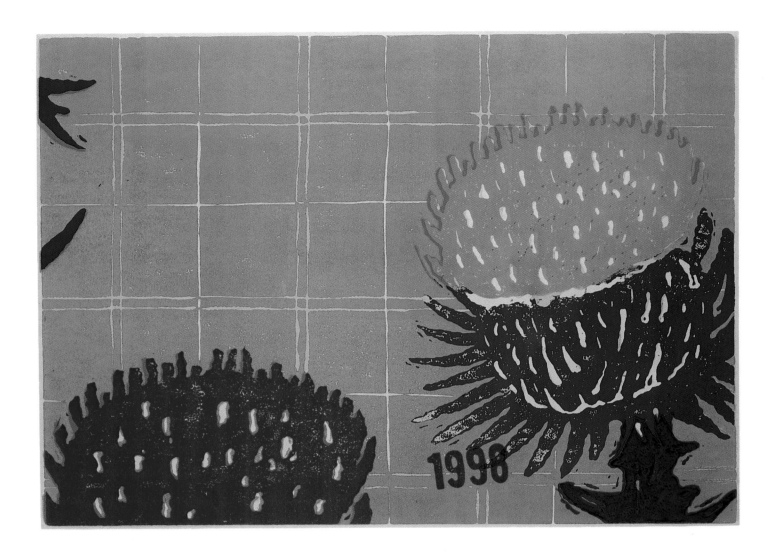

title
New Scottish
Writing

medium
Lino print

purpose of work
Book Cover

brief
To produce a cover
illustration for a
diverse collection
of contemporary
Scottish writing

commissioned by
Becky Glibbery

company
Harper
Collins/Flamingo

lizzie harper

Top Floot Flat
11 Ullet Road
Liverpool
L17 3DP

t. 0151 733 5209
m. 07714 246447
email. lizzie@consciousdesign.demon.co.uk

title
Canada Goose

medium
Watercolour

purpose of work
Information panel

brief
Full colour
illustration of
Canada Geese for
identification
purposes

commissioned by
Mike Graham

company
Towneley Museum,
Burnley

title
Ne-Ne (Hawaiian
Goose)

medium
Watercolour

purpose of work
Information panel

brief
Illustrate the Ne Ne
in situ

commissioned by
Nicky Greek

company
Bolton Park
Services

lizzie harper

Top Floot Flat
11 Ullet Road
Liverpool
L17 3DP

t. 0151 733 5209
m. 07714 246447
email. lizzie@consciousdesign.demon.co.uk

GENERAL BOOKS

title
Cuckoo Wasp
medium
Watercolour
purpose of work
Insect identification
brief
Scaled up
illustration of
cuckoo wasp
specimen

ian massey

12 Gloucester Avenue
Levenshulme
Manchester
M19 3WT

t. 0161 224 0079
email. ian@masmot.demon.co.uk

title
Moving Mountains

medium
Mixed media on paper

purpose of work
Book jacket design for "Moving Mountains" by John Waters

brief
To produce a cover for a book detailing the Christian ministry of Father Simaan, whose congregation are a community of impoverished litter collectors living near Cairo

commissioned by
Nikki Bovis-Coulter

company
SPCK

james marsh

21 Elms Road
London
SW4 9ER

t. 020 7622 9530
f. 020 7498 6851

title
The Owl Service
medium
Acrylics on canvas
purpose of work
Book jacket

brief
Open brief for anthropomorphic ghost story - Collins Classics
commissioned by
Mike Watts
company
Harper Collins

sarah perkins

37e Guinness Court
Snowfields
London
SE1 3SX

t. 020 7378 1510
t. 020 7357 6114
f. 020 7357 6442
email. mum-dad.co.uk

114

GB

title
Through a Glass
Darkly

medium
Mixed Media

purpose of work
Book Jacket

brief
Magical and
abstract but
otherwise free
- the book

Commissioned by
Orion Publishing

Agent
The Inkshed
98 Columbia Road
London
E2 7QB
t. 020 7613 2323

fiona mcnab

10 Gloucester Street
Brighton
East Sussex
BN1 4EW

t. 01273 683 371
email. fionamcnab@line.net

GENERAL BOOKS

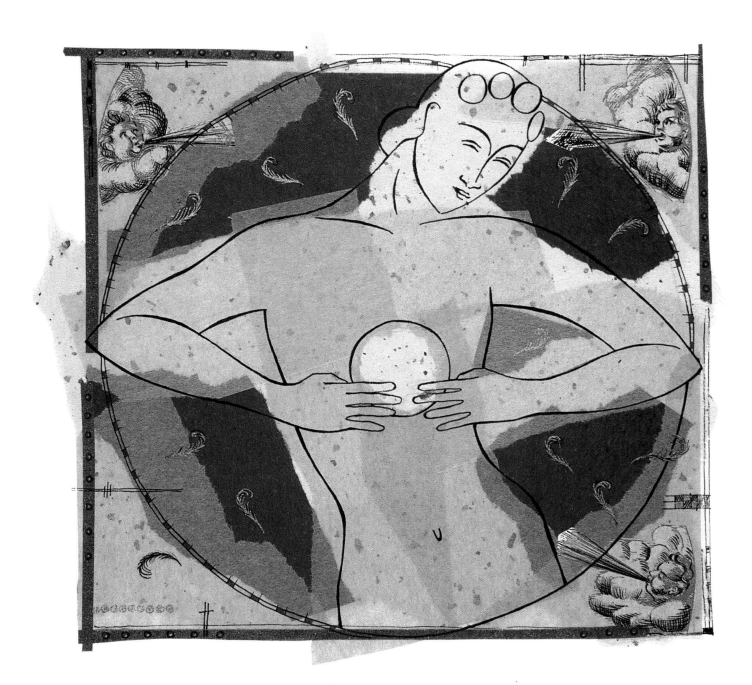

title
Breath

medium
Collage and
gouache

purpose of work
Book jacket for the
'breath book'

brief
To illustrate an
androgynous
person holding
their diaphragm,
including a feeling
of relaxation and
lightness of being

david rooney

The Loft House
Woodbrook
Bray
County Wicklow
Ireland

t. 00 353 1 282 5635
email. lofthaus@iol.ie

title
The Sniper

medium
Scraper board

purpose of work
Book illustration
for Irish Short
Stories

brief
Irish civil war story
tells of a sniper
who unwittingly
shoots his brother.
This early scene
shows the death of
an informant

Commissioned by
Joe Whitlock-
Blundell

Company
The Folio Society

title
Korea

medium
Scraper board

purpose of work
Book illustration
for Irish Short
Stories

brief
A son's complex
relationship with
father is illustrated
while eel fishing,
where it is revealed
that father
suggested son
might join the US
marines and go to
fight in Korea

Commissioned by
Joe Whitlock-
Blundell

Company
The Folio Society

david rooney

The Loft House
Woodbrook
Bray
County Wicklow
Ireland
t. 00 353 1 282 5635
email. lofthaus@iol.ie

title
Mr Sing My Heart's
Delight

medium
Scraper board

purpose of work
Book illustration
for Irish Short
Stories

brief
Indian travelling
salesman visits a
widow in remote
west of Ireland
setting

Commissioned by
Joe Whitlock-
Blundell

Company
The Folio Society

louise weir

Monster
Studio 32
10 Martello Street
London E8 3PE

t. 020 7923 9639
f. 020 7923 9639
m. 07966 284 090
email. monsters@.monsters.co.uk
web. www.monsters.co.uk

title
One Day as a Tiger

medium
Acrylic

purpose of work
Wrap around book
cover

brief
To produce an
image as evocative
and humorous as
the book, focusing
on Irish perspective
and relationship
between farmer
and sheep

commissioned by
Pascale Hutton

company
Vintage Books

agent
Monster
Studio 32
10 Martello Street
London
E8 3PE
t. 020 7923 9639

pierre-paul pariseau

3997 St Dominique St., 2
Montreal
Quebec, Canada
H2W 2A4

t. 001 514 849 2964
f. 001 514 843 4808

medium
Photo collage

purpose of work
Book jacket

brief
The book is a diary
about the making
of the BBC
documentary
"Waiting for
Harvey"

commissioned by
Robert
Hollingsworth

company
Random House
UK Ltd

agent
The Organisation
69 Caledonian Rd
Kings Cross
London N1 9BT
t. 020 7833 8268

paul wearing

Unit B4
Metropolitan Wharf
Wapping Wall
London
E1 9SS

t. 020 7481 4653
f. 020 7481 4654
email. paulwearing@illustrator.demon.co.uk

title
Dubliners

medium
Digital

purpose of work
Book jacket

brief
Evoke the feeling
of book and period
in which it was
written without
literal reference to
imagery in text

commissioned by
Caz Hildebrand

company
Random House

Unit B4
Metropolitan Wharf
Wapping Wall
London
E1 9SS

t. 020 7481 4653
f. 020 7481 4654
email. paulwearing@illustrator.demon.co.uk

121
GB

title
Finnegans Wake

medium
Digital

purpose of work
Book jacket

brief
Evoke the feeling
of book and period
in which it was
written without
literal reference to
imagery in text

commissioned by
Caz Hildebrand

company
Random House

paul wearing

Unit B4
Metropolitan Wharf
Wapping Wall
London
E1 9SS

t. 020 7481 4653
f. 020 7481 4654
email. paulwearing@illustrator.demon.co.uk

title
Ulysses

medium
Digital

purpose of work
Book jacket

brief
Evoke the feeling
of book and period
in which it was
written without
literal reference to
imagery in text

commissioned by
Caz Hildebrand

company
Random House

stan chow

18 Brydges Road
Marple
Stockport
SK6 7RA

t. 0161 427 2668
f. 0161 427 2668
m. 0961 396 502

title
Hot Sex Tips

medium
Acrylic

purpose of work
Book jacket

brief
To create a sexy
but sophisticated
image for a book
cover for
Cosmopolitan
series entitled "Hot
Sex Tips - How to
Have Him Begging
for More"

commissioned by
Sonia Doby

company
Harper Collins

agent
Central Illustration
Agency
36 Wellington
Street
London
WC2E 7ED
t. 020 7240 8925
f. 020 7836 1177

judges   **Matthew Axe** / Designer / John Lewis Partnership

David Freeman / Creative Director / Enterprise IG Ltd

Conor Brady / Art Director / Decca Records Co Ltd

Chloe Cheese / Illustrator

Illustration by Nelly Dimitranova +44 (0)20 7284 2334

print & design

Print & design

It has been particularly pleasing in recent years to see so much contemporary illustration appearing on Royal Mail postage stamps. With a 50 million print run and worldwide audience the illustrator has a unique opportunity to showcase their work. This year's section winner, Sara Fanelli, was chosen to illustrate one of the Millennium series.

Sara's portfolio was initially requested by Barry Robinson, the Design Director at the Royal Mail. 'After my portfolio had gone in I received a request to attend a meeting which was to explain the Millennium series project,' says Sara. Barry Robinson and Mike Dempsey of CDT, who were handling the project, commissioned forty-eight artists for the ongoing series with each image revolving around a different themed story. Sara was asked to illustrate the invention of the bicycle, its links to the emancipation of women and the benefits to the environment. After discussing the background to the story she was given a written brief explaining how until the invention of the bicycle women had to rely on men for their transportation.

'I was quite intimidated when at first faced with such an important commission but I soon found my main image of the flying woman holding on to the handlebars. I then drew up two or three variations on a layout which were all quite similar but with different details – one was wearing trousers for instance.'
The sketches were then submitted.

'Originally I had the Queen's bust on a wheel as well which they asked to be removed but they were mostly concerned with the detailing of the bike. It had to be exact. Eventually they put me in touch with an expert on the subject who supplied me with reference.'

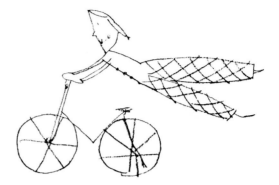

The inclusion of a small dog on wheels was a welcome addition. 'I was expecting the dog would have to go', says Sara. 'I had recently finished some work on dogs which is why I included him, but also because I like to relate my own work with a project.'

The next stage was a colour rough which was hand painted in gouache with various collaged elements. This was forwarded, with her portfolio as backup, for committee approval. The go-ahead was given with four weeks to complete the artwork.

After deciding on a size of roughly 20 cms square the background was painted in gouache with the wheels rendered in black with pen on an overlay. Collaged elements of the figure were painted separately on paper before being cut out and pasted in position.

'The paper needs to be thick enough to cast a shadow when photographed – I like the sort of enhanced 3D quality it gives the picture.'

Additional layers were prepared for the dog's leash and one for the silver on the arrows, wing tips and type.

'It was a wonderful job to work on,' says Sara, 'I still can't quite believe I've done it.'

The 26p stamp entitled *Millennium Liberation* was issued on February 2nd 1999.

Flat 11
Howitt Close
Howitt Road
London
NW3 4LX

t. 020 7483 2544
f. 020 7483 2544

title
Liberation by Bike

medium
Collage

purpose of work
Millennium stamp

brief
Celebrating the
invention of the
bicycle

commissioned by
Barry Robinson

company
Royal Mail

sara fanelli

Flat 11
Howitt Close
Howitt Road
London
NW3 4LX

t. 020 7483 2544
f. 020 7483 2544

128
GB

title
Come round to
George Square
medium
Collage
purpose of work
Brochure cover -
Edinburgh
University Theatre
Festival

brief
Image to advertise
the venue of the
theatre festival
(George Square
Theatre)
commissioned by
Mike Samouelle
company
University of
Edinburgh

title
Chaplaincy Centre
medium
Collage
purpose of work
Brochure cover -
Edinburgh
University Theatre
Festival

brief
Image to advertise
the venue of the
theatre festival
(Chaplaincy Centre)
commissioned by
Mike Samouelle
company
University of
Edinburgh

michael bramman

104 Dudley Court
Upper Berkeley
Street
London
W1H 7PJ

t. 020 7723 3564
f. 020 7723 3564

title
The Chase
medium
Acrylic
purpose of work
Cards, prints and
posters for sale
and promotion of
gallery
brief
Work to reflect a
visit to the Cantel
commissioned by
Sue & Nigel Atkins
company
La Galerie du Don

title
The Forest Trail
medium
Acrylic

michael clark

Mount Charles House
36 Mount Charles Crescent
Alloway
Ayrshire
Scotland
KA7 4NY

t. 01292 440254
f. 01292 440254

title
The Christening Dress

medium
Oil on paper

purpose of work
Greetings card

brief
Fresh image for new baby girl or christening card

commissioned by
Julia Woodmansterne

company
Woodmansterne Publications Ltd

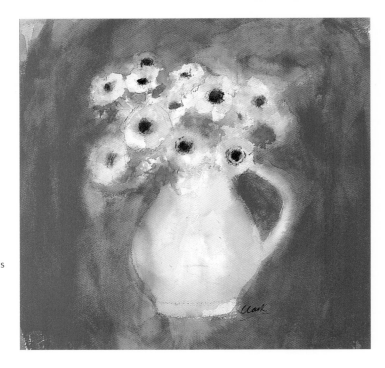

title
Tickled Pink

medium
Watercolour

purpose of work
Greetings card

brief
Cheerful upbeat image for use on birthday and mother's day cards

commissioned by
Julia Woodmansterne

company
Woodmansterne Publications Ltd

PRINT & DESIGN

title
A Day at the Races
medium
Ink, watercolour
purpose of work
Double page
illustration for
Goodwood
Magazine
brief
To capture the
atmosphere of a
race day during the
summer

commissioned by
Goodwood
Magazine
company
West London
Design Company
agent
Arena
144 Royal College
Street
London
NW1 0TA
t. 020 7267 9661

madeleine floyd

5 Beaumont
Crescent
London
W14 9LX
t. 020 7610 2381
f. 020 7610 2381

132
GB

title
Elephant

medium
Ink and
watercolour

purpose of work
Image for range of
animal cards

brief
To produce 6
images of wild
animals for new
range of cards to
be sold worldwide

commissioned by
Art Angels

title
The Whole Mess -
Part II (by DJ Noize)

medium
Mixed Media / 3-
dimensional
construction

purpose of work
Record sleeve for
DJ Noize

brief
To illustrate the
former world
champion's second
album cover,
incorporating
elements of a
specific culture

commissioned by
Rita Records

agent
Arena
144 Royal College
Street
London
NW1 0TA
t. 020 7267 9661

title
Christmas Day

medium
Gouache

purpose of work
Illustrate article in
WPP Atticus

brief
Depict how
different social
groups spend
Christmas Day.
(Series of 3)

commissioned by
David Freeman

company
Enterprise IG

agent
Heart
1 Tysoe Street
London
EC1R 4SA
t. 020 7278 8522
f. 020 7278 7660

andy lovell

See Agent

title	**commissioned by**
Music in TV	David Freeman
advertising	**company**
medium	Enterprise IG
Gouache	**agent**
purpose of work	Heart
Illustrate article in	1 Tysoe Street
WPP Atticus	London
brief	EC1R 4SA
Depict the	t. 020 7278 4447
importance of	
music in TV	
advertising	

sue clark

See Agent

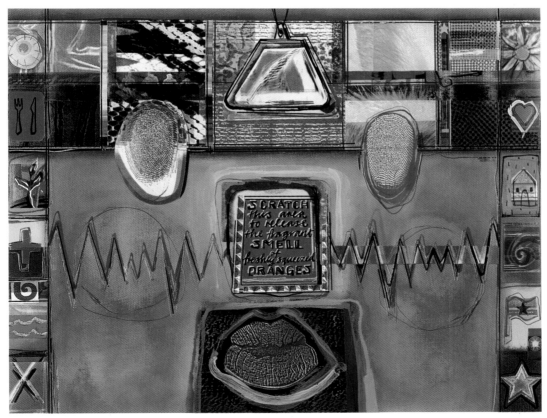

title	**commissioned by**
The Senses	David Freeman
medium	**company**
Mixed Media	Enterprise IG
purpose of work	**agent**
Illustrate article in	Eastwing
WPP Atticus	98 Columbia Road
brief	London
Depict that all the	E2 7QB
senses come into	t. 020 7613 5580
play in a consumer	
purchasing decision	

simon stern

19 Corringham Road
London
NW11 7BS

t. 020 8458 8250
f. 020 8458 8250

title
Hear, See, Look,
No Evil

medium
Ink, wash

purpose of work
Illustrate article in
WPP Atticus

brief
Depict that
consumers apply a
"moral filter" to
advertising

commissioned by
David Freeman

company
Enterprise IG

agent
The Inkshed
98 Columbia Road
London
E2 7QB
t. 020 7613 2323

---

ian whadcock

8 Middlehills
Macclesfield
Cheshire
SK11 7EQ

t. 01625 618 068
f. 01625 618 068

title
Brand Erosion

medium
Digital

purpose of work
Illustrate article in
WPP Atticus

brief
Depict how brands
can be damaged by
incorrect use of
promotions

commissioned by
David Freeman

company
Enterprise IG

agent
Eastwing
98 Columbia Road
London
E2 7QB
t. 020 7613 5580

jerry malone

37b Fonnereau
Road
Ipswich
Suffolk
IP1 3JH

t. 01473 288668

title
Butterfly Man

medium
Ink

purpose of work
Illustrate concept
for Enterprise IG
"Issues" - Brand
alignment

brief
Depict a character
who has been
"enlightened"

commissioned by
Tom Crew

company
Enterprise IG

title
Flower Men

medium
Ink

purpose of work
Illustrate concept
for Enterprise IG
"Issues" - Brand
alignment

brief
Depict two people
speaking the same
language

commissioned by
Tom Crew

company
Enterprise IG

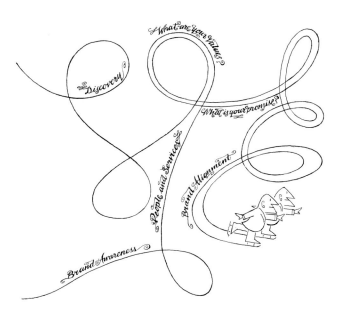

title
Ice Skaters

medium
Ink

purpose of work
Illustrate concept
for Enterprise IG
"Issues" - Brand
alignment

brief
Depict the concept
of alignment

commissioned by
Tom Crew

company
Enterprise IG

david smith

65 Breech Lane
Walton-on-the-Hill
Tadworth
Surrey
KT20 7SJ

t. 01737 814 189
f. 01737 814 190

138

GB

title
Cyber Attack

medium
Mixed Media

purpose of work
Illustrate article in
WPP Atticus

brief
Depict how the
Internet is being
used by pressure
groups

commissioned by
David Freeman

company
Enterprise IG

elena gomez

Stonelands
Portsmouth Road
Milford, Godalming
Surrey, GU8 5DR

t 01483 423876
t. 01483 426607
f. 01483 423935

title
Hen House

medium
Acrylic

purpose of work
Print for Art
Group's own range

brief
Develop a bright
print on a theme of
previous bright
work for kitchen or
children's room

commissioned by
Janie Markham

company
The Art Group Ltd

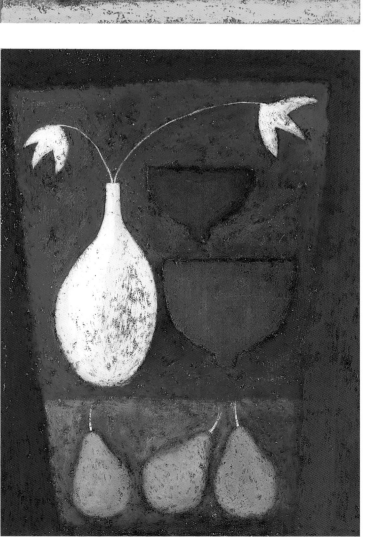

title
Pears on Blue

medium
Acrylic

purpose of work
Print for Art
Group's own range

brief
Develop a print
from a theme of
previous still life
work

commissioned by
Janie Markham

company
The Art Group Ltd

nelly dimitranova

Top Flat
33 Savernake Road
London
NW3 2JU

t. 020 7284 2334
f. 020 7284 2334
pager. 07654 290 890

140
GB

title
Chrysler Coffee
medium
Acrylic and crayon
purpose of work
Poster
brief
To depict the
morning
atmosphere in New
York
agent
Eastwing
98 Columbia Road
London
E2 7QB
t. 020 7613 5580

brian grimwood

CIA
36 Wellington Street
London WC2E 7BD

t. 020 7836 0391
f. 01273 564 979
m. 0402 955 388
pager. 01523 177 959
email. grimwood@briangrimwood.com

title
Wheelbarrow

medium
Acrylic

purpose of work
Beer label -
exhibition
promotion

brief
Exhibition
promotion

agent
Central Illustration
Agency
36 Wellington Street
London
WC2E 7BD
t. 020 7240 8925
f. 020 7836 1177

david gillooley

The Signal Box
Shelley
Huddersfield
Yorkshire
HD8 8LZ

t. 01484 608779

t. 01484 536553

email. sigbox_dg@tinyonline.co.uk

title
York Minster

medium
Pen and Ink

purpose of work
Information

brief
An unusual but
current view of the
minister avoiding
scaffolding

commissioned by
Michele Adams

company
F-Sharp

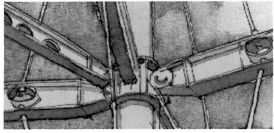

David Gillooley
01484 608009

elaine hackett

2 Heatherside
Cottages
Montgomery Hill
Frankby
Wirral
Merseyside
CH48 1NQ

t. 0151 625 6701

title
I Saw Three Ships

medium
Acrylic ink and
pencil

purpose of work
Christmas card to
be printed

brief
To illustrate the
song "I Saw Three
Ships" using an
animal and
decorative waves

Commissioned by
S. Nichol

alison jay

14 Ingersoll Road
London
W12 7BD

t. 020 8749 2264

title
The Balloon of
Experience

medium
Alkyd and varnish
on paper

purpose of work
Times Literary
supplement
calendar

brief
To illustrate a
quote by Henry
James for April

commissioned by
McWilliams
Partnership

company
T.L.S.

agent
The Organisation
69 Caledonian
Road
London
N1 9BT
t. 020 7833 8268

satoshi kambayashi

Flat 2
40 Tisbury Road
Hove
East Sussex
BN3 3BA
t. 01273 771539
f. 01273 771539
email. satoshi.k@virgin.net

title
It's Mine!

medium
Line and wash

purpose of work
Christmas Card

brief
Create a Christmas
card image for the
Guardian

commissioned by
Mark Porter

company
The Guardian

title
'IT' Management
School

medium
Line and wash

purpose of work
Illustrating a
corporate
newsletter/brochure

brief
A university style
course providing an
education in IT
Management and
Multi-Dimensional
Management

commissioned by
Dominic Finnigan

company
SPY Design

agent
Ian Flemming &
Associates
t. 020 7734 8701

james marsh

21 Elms Road
London
SW4 9ER

t. 020 7622 9530
f. 020 7498 6851

title
Visionary

medium
Acrylics on canvas

purpose of work
Corporate brochure

brief
To illustrate the
title for brochure.
One in a series of
eight by different
artists

commissioned by
Chris Hyde

company
Phildrew Ventures

andrew kulman

110 Scalpcliffe Road
Burton upon Trent
East Staffordshire
DE15 9AB

t. 01283 569989
f. 01283 569989
email. andrew.kulman@uce.ac.uk

title	**commissioned by**
Noah's Ark	Jorg Birker Design
medium	**agent**
Lino cut	CIA
purpose of work	36 Wellington
Announcement card	Street
/ promotional	London
brief	WC2E 7BD
Personal	t. 020 7836 1106
interpretation of	
Noah's ark	

title	**commissioned by**
Some	Lynn Trickett /
medium	Brian Webb
Silkscreen from	
linocut	**company**
	Trickett & Webb
purpose of work	**agent**
Calendar image	CIA
brief	36 Wellington
Artist interpreted	Street
the word 'some' as	London
part of a 52 word	WC2E 7BD
story	t. 020 7836 1106

mark mcconnell

Court Yard Studio
Panther House
38 Mount Pleasant
London
WC1X 0AP

t. 020 7833 4113
f. 020 7833 3064

PRINT & DESIGN

title
Deeper, Wider,
Smoother, Shit

medium
Acrylic

purpose of work
Illustration for CD
cover

brief
To portray artist as
a D.J. in a club

commissioned by
Doug Hart

company
Recordings of
Substance

clare yull mackie

21A Ursula Street
London
SW11 3DW

t. 020 7223 8649
f. 020 7223 4119

title
January 1999
medium
Watercolour & ink
purpose of work
Calendar

brief
Completely open
brief to produce
any image I wanted
for their self
promotion calendar
commissioned by
Alain L'Achatre
company
Vue sur La Ville

john o'leary • irma irsara

16b Charteris Road
Finsbury Park
London
N4 3AB

t. 020 7272 2521
f. 020 7272 2521

title
Treasure Chest

medium
Dyed paper pulp,
relief printing

purpose of work
Hand-made
greetings cards,
one of a series
featuring hearts

brief
Design a series of
hand-made cards
suitable for
different occasions
and open to
different
interpretations

Commissioned by
Steven Jenkins

Company
Festival

kate newington

30 Saltoun Road
London
SW2 1EP

t. 020 7274 1418
f. 020 7274 1418
e. knewington@yahoo.co.uk

title
Laura, Hector and
Daisy

medium
Collage

purpose of work
Commissioned
privately by Jaine
Greene

brief
To make a collage
portrait of Jaine
Greene's three
children

chris orr & associates

11 Portland Street
Southampton
SO14 7EB

t. 023 8033 3991
f. 023 8033 3995
email: art@chrisorr.co.uk
www.chrisorr.co.uk

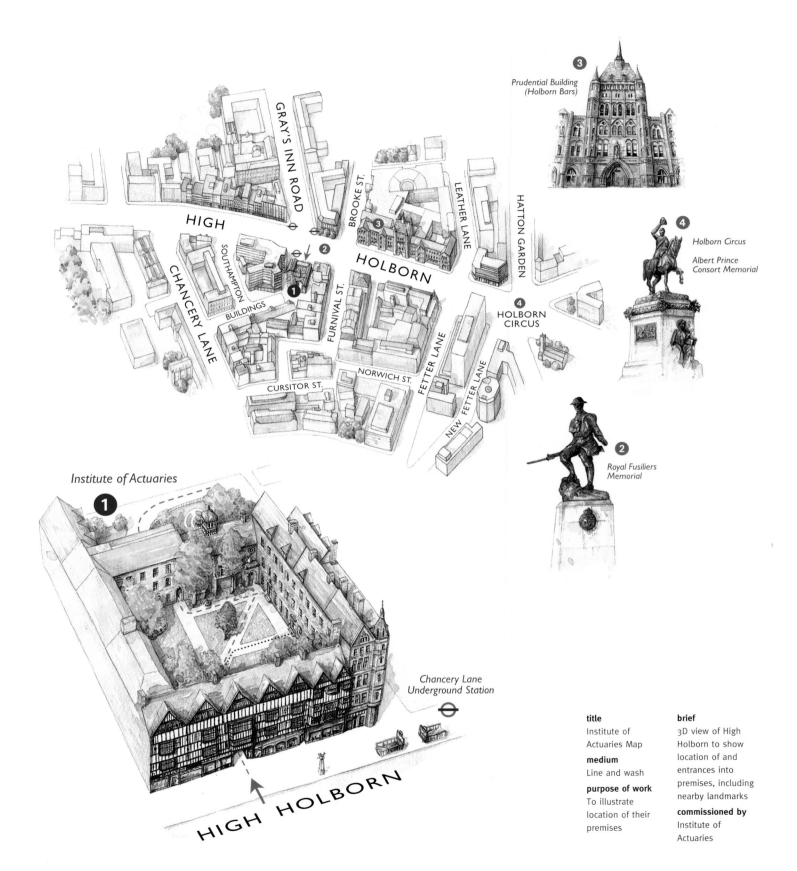

title	brief
Institute of Actuaries Map	3D view of High Holborn to show location of and entrances into premises, including nearby landmarks
medium	
Line and wash	
purpose of work	**commissioned by**
To illustrate location of their premises	Institute of Actuaries

sarah perkins

37e Guinness Court
Snowfields
London
SE1 3SX

t. 020 7378 1510
t. 020 7357 6114
f. 020 7357 6442
email. mum-dad.co.uk

title
All Things Nice

medium
Mixed Media

purpose of work
Greetings card for
mum

brief
Colourful, retro,
aimed at mums

Commissioned by
The Art Group

Agent
The Inkshed
98 Columbia Road
London
E2 7QB
t. 020 7613 2323

piero (hernan pierini)

5 Bedford House
61 Lisson Street
London
NW1 5DD

t. 020 7724 4592
email. piero@dial.pipex.com

PRINT & DESIGN

title
Japan-Sports

medium
Watercolour

purpose of work
Tourism brochure

brief
To create images
about Japanese
culture

commissioned by
Laura Santamaria

company
A.M.S. Applied
Marketing
Solutions

paul powis

Four Seasons
Battenhall Avenue
Worcester
WR5 2HW

t. 01905 357 563
f. 01905 357 563

title
Mustard Fields

medium
Acrylic

purpose of work
Greetings card

brief
Selected from
portfolio

commissioned by
Dominic Seckler

company
Nouvelles Images

nik ramage

99A Newington Green Road
London
N1 4QY

t. 020 7354 8355
m. 0976 314 302

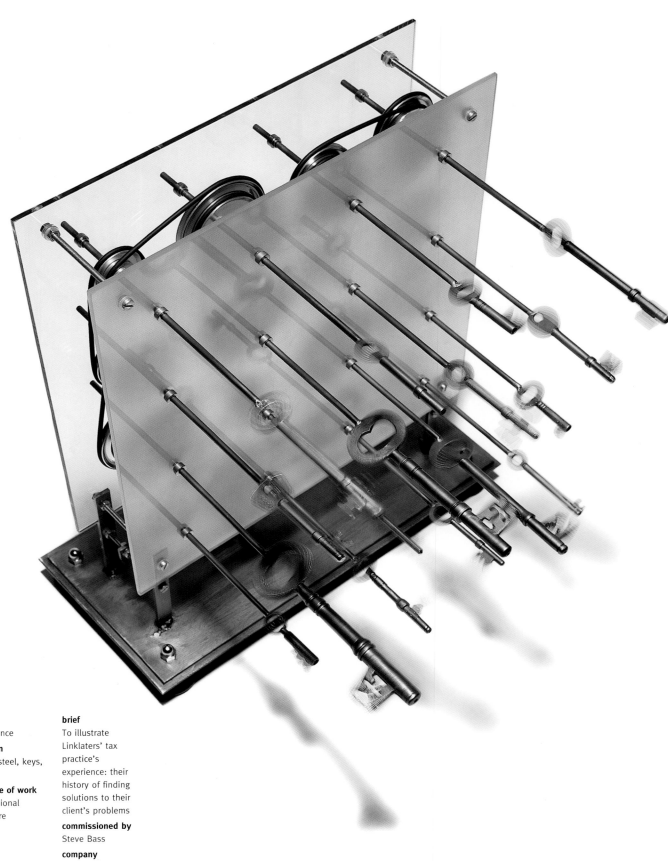

title
Experience

medium
Glass, steel, keys, motor

purpose of work
Promotional brochure

brief
To illustrate Linklaters' tax practice's experience: their history of finding solutions to their client's problems

commissioned by
Steve Bass

company
Saatchi & Saatchi Design

peter warner

Peter Warner's Studio
Hillside Road
Tatsfield
Kent
TN16 2NH

t 01959 577270
f. 01959 541414
m. 07958 531538
email. thestudio@peterwarner.co.uk
www.peterwarner.co.uk

159

GB

title
Asda Tiger
medium
Watercolour
purpose of work
Icon for pet food
packaging and POS

brief
To create an active,
cheeky,
mischievous, red
tabby cat character
lying on a ribbon
device, playing
with a ball of wool
and appearing
caught in the act
commissioned by
Chris Wilson
company
Elmwood Design
Limited

alan young

2 Chapel Cottages
Dunks Green
Tonbridge
Kent
TN11 9SF

t. 01732 810652
f. 01622 621100

160

GB

title
Jazz Piquant

medium
Watercolour

purpose of work
CD Cover

brief
Image to reflect
selection of songs
about France or by
French Composers

commissioned by
Martin Hall Nicholls

company
33 Records

stephen waterhouse

2A Norwood Grove
Birkenshaw
Bradford
West Yorkshire
BD11 2NP

t. 01274 877111
f. 01274 877111
mobile. 07971 347856

title
Three Ships
medium
Acrylic
purpose of work
Christmas card
brief
To take the title
"Three Ships" and
produce a
contemporary fun
image
commissioned by
Sue Waddicor
company
Webb Ivory Ltd

title
When the Clock
Strikes Twelve
medium
Acrylic
purpose of work
Fine art print for
the millennium
commissioned by
Shane Henstock
company
Rowan Fine Art &
Editions Ltd

judges   **Bill Butcher** / Illustrator

David Male / Agent / Inkshed

Cathy Caldwell / Lecturer / Central St Martins College of Art & Design

Glen Baxter / Illustrator

Illustration by Anna Steinberg +44 (0)20 8964 1069

student

Student

Section winner: Jonathon Cusick Knit One, Pearl Two

Design process by Anna Steinberg

Jonathon Cusick's image *Knit One, Pearl Two* formed part of his final year show on the theme, 'All Things British'. He wrote lists to encourage ideas which he describes as a 'mental dribble' including London buses, taxis, knitting and tea. He is fond of pensioners and caricatures generally yet Pearl is apparently not based on any particular sweet old lady. It was the highest scoring submission in the Student section, which had hundreds of entries.

Jonathon's art education consisted of a BTEC National diploma followed by a first in illustration at Birminham Institute of Art and Design. His successes have been numerous and impressive. In 1995 he won the Young Cartoonist of the Year award sponsored by The Times and British Cartoonists Association. He won the first prize in the D&AD student awards for illustration in 1998 and had five entries selected in *Images 23*, in addition to the student prize this year. To date clients have included The Guardian, Harper Collins and BHX Advertising as well as many private commissions for caricatures.

At college he already had a practical attitude to the profession and he credits this partly to the encouragement of his tutor Andrew Kulman. He is an enthusiastic competition enterer, particularly enthusiastic in light of recent events and has been keen to contact people within the industry whom he admires for help. His painting surfaces are a development from a tip from the 'school of Paul Slater' and comprise layers of fabric, PVA, gesso and stretched paper. Jonathon is quite critical of his own work but it must be said he has been out-numbered.

jonathan cusick

10 Wynyates
Sageside
Tamworth
Staffordshire
B79 7UP

t. 01827 50003
f. 01827 50003

165

GB

title
Knit One, Pearl
Two

medium
Acrylic

purpose of work
Self promotional

brief
Part of a series
depicting British
activities, in this
case Knitting

jonathan cusick

10 Wynyates
Sageside
Tamworth
Staffordshire
B79 7UP

t. 01827 50003
f. 01827 50003

166
GB

title
The Great 'W.G.'

medium
Acrylic

purpose of work
Self promotional

brief
To produce a portrait of W.G. Grace in an inventive and personal way. From a series featuring British culture and heritage

jonathan cusick

10 Wynyates
Sageside
Tamworth
Staffordshire
B79 7UP

t. 01827 50003
f. 01827 50003

title
What goes on
inside the Queen's
Head

medium
Oils

purpose of work
Self promotional
exhibition piece

brief
To produce a large
and intriguing
exhibition piece.
From a series
featuring British
culture; this
example visualises
Cockney rhyming
slang

jonathan cusick

10 Wynyates
Sageside
Tamworth
Staffordshire
B79 7UP

t. 01827 50003
f. 01827 50003

168

GB

title
The Tea Ceremony
medium
Acrylic
purpose of work
Advertising
brief
To produce ads for
tea featuring
builders. This
example
reinterprets the
Japanese tea
ceremony

jonathan cusick

10 Wynyates
Sageside
Tamworth
Staffordshire
B79 7UP

t. 01827 50003
f. 01827 50003

title
Milk, no sugar
medium
Oils
purpose of work
Self promotional

title
The Birthday
Beerhead
medium
Acrylic
purpose of work
Greetings card (for
18-25's)

7 Netherfield Road
London
N12 8DP

t. 020 8922 7800
m. 07974 749 889

Pentagram ★ **award winner:** *The Pentagram Award*

title
Reasons why not
to like bed time
story characters
medium
Mixed Media
purpose of work
Major project
brief
Book jacket

title
A Pair of Unlikeable
Wizards
medium
Mixed Media
purpose of work
Major project
brief
Illustration for
'Reasons why not
to like bed time
story characters'

title
You Half Turn into
a Zebra
medium
Acrylic
purpose of work
Self-promotional
brief
On your way to the
shops...

david john atkinson

46 Herbert Street
Loughborough
Leics
LE11 1NX

t. 01509 550148
m. 07977 968999

STUDENTS

title
Crossing

medium
Watercolour

purpose of work
Student work

brief
The theatrical zoo

john bates

27 Faraday Road
Welling
Kent
DA16 2ET

t. 020 8304 0707
m. 07939 233 984

172
GB

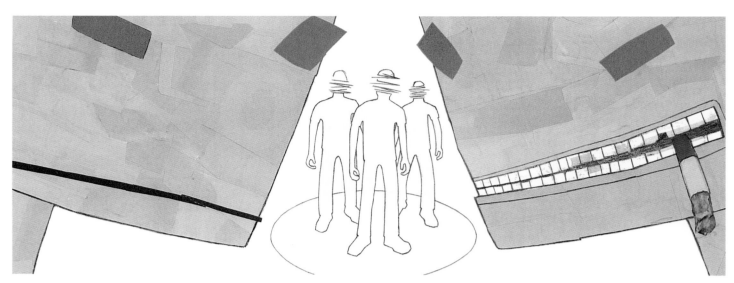

title
Earth vs Space
Casuals

medium
Collage, acrylic

purpose of work
Personal promotion

brief
Illustration from an
Irvine Welsh short
story "The
Rosewell Incident"

title
Head transplant,
Sir? No problem

medium
Collage, emulsion

purpose of work
Personal promotion

brief
To illustrate recent
reports that head
transplants could
soon become
reality, and to
show possible side
effects

roger bunting

8 Sunningdale
Close
Walton
Chesterfield
Derbyshire
S40 3JA

t. 01246 206271
email. r.d.bunting@talk21.com

title
Triumphant Return

medium
Acrylics, mixed
media

purpose of work
Book Illustration

brief
One of a set of four
illustrations
depicting Lewis
Carroll's poem
"Jabberwocky"

james brown

43 Springthorpe Green
Erdington
Birmingham
B24 0TN
t. 0121 350 8561

title
The Greedy Wolf

medium
Acrylic and
watercolour

purpose of work
Children's
storybook cards

brief
Create cards for
children using story
book characters

title
The Much Does a
Head Weigh?

medium
Inks

purpose of work
To make fun
images

brief
To make an image
for the phrase
'light-headed'

emily burton

1 Oak Road
Reigate
Surrey
RH2 0BP

t. 01737 248508

Title
Jazz Cafe

medium
Pen and Ink

purpose of work
One of a series of
drawings to fit brief

brief
To produce a
"Rough Guide to
Bath" based on
location drawing

madeleine cole

4 Park Close
Cossington
Near Bridgwater
Somerset
TA7 8LG

t. 01278 722995
m. 07974 714249

176
GB

title
The Rush Hour
Business Man

medium
Photographic /
Collage

purpose of work
College coursework

brief
Open brief - to
show the change in
attitude of the
everyday man
when it comes to
rush hour

title
Airport Security

medium
Photographic
montage

purpose of work
College coursework

brief
An observational
study of any
location of your
choice

berengere ducoms

21 Claverdale Road
London
SW2 2DJ

t. 020 8671 1411
f. 07070 601 835

title
Awakening
Thalasso Therapy

medium
Pencil and
computer

purpose of work
Personal work

brief
Inspiration from an
article in French
magazine

richard johnson

273 London Road
Storeygate
Leicester
LE2 3BE

t. 07931 136235
m. 01263 821 219
email. richj@hotmail.com

178
GB

title
If life gives you
lemons, then make
lemonade

medium
Acrylic

purpose of work
College project

brief
To interpret and
illustrate the quote
above

title
Rounding Up

medium
Acrylic

purpose of work
Editorial

brief
To produce an
image illustrating a
new computer
program which
reads and sorts
files for the user

title
A Taste of Italy

medium
Acrylic

purpose of work
Advertisement

brief
To produce an
image illustrating
Italian food and
culture which
should work as
part of set of food
hall posters

virginia lee

7 Netherfield Road
London
N12 8DP

t. 020 8922 7800
m. 0797 4252 737

title
Inner Seasons

medium
Pastel on paper

purpose of work
Major project

brief
One of a series of
illustrations for a
book describing a
young girl entering
puberty and
realising her
physical changes in
nature around her

title
Waiting for
Redemption

medium
Modelling clay,
acrylic and papier
machÈ

purpose of work
Personal project

brief
To look at fairy tale
characters and the
problems they may
encounter being in
their form

roberto greene

c/o 60 Clubley Estate
St. Helier
Jersey
JE2 3LF

t. 01534 25255
email. positivejunk@hotmail.com

180

GB

title
Down Down in
China Town

medium
Acrylic paint, ink
and gold pen

purpose of work
College student
work

brief
An illustration to
accompany an
extract from a story
of my own entitled
"Down Down in
China Town"

jan martin

32 Albert Park Place
Montpelier
Bristol
BS6 5ND

t. 0117 908 1675
t. 0117 954 1342

title
Hunting

medium
Collage

purpose of work
Student course
work

brief
Self directed

c/o Illustration
School of
Communications
Royal College of Art
Kensington Gore
London
SW7 2EU

m. 07974 375 515

Pentagram

★ **award winner:** *The Pentagram Award*

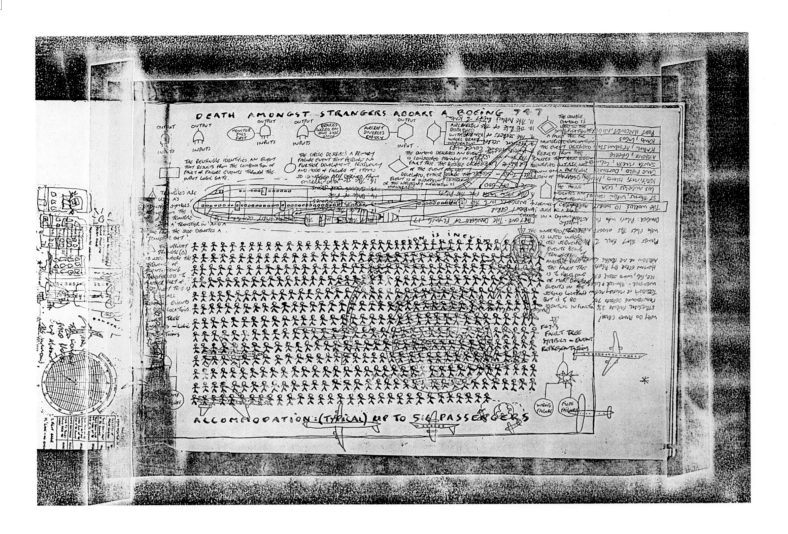

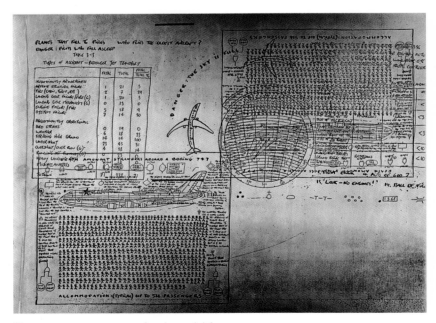

title
Death Amongst
Strangers +
Airplane Crash Data
medium
Mixed Media

purpose of work
2 in a series of
images inspired by
a passage in the
Julian Barnes novel
"Staring at the
Sun"

brief
A depiction of the
character's
paranoid dialogue
concerning
mechanical failures
in airplanes and
the consequential
loss of life

title
Vigilante
medium
Pen and ink
purpose of work
For a proposed
editorial article

brief
To illustrate an
article regarding
the ethics of
vigilante justice

eva tatcheva

80 Waverley Road
Harrow
Middlesex
HA2 9RD

t. 020 8866 3586
f. 020 8866 3586

STUDENTS

title
Vanilla Ice-cream
Mania

medium
Mixed Media

purpose of work
Self promotional

brief
Illustration for
article about
European ice-cream
consumption

ella grace burfoot

3 Cromer Road
Ingworth
Norwich
Norfolk
NR11 6PJ
t. 01263 732001

title
People on Earth
Can't See Me...
medium
Dr Marten's, inks,
mono-printing
purpose of work
Children's book for
the solar eclipse 99

brief
Commissioned
book "Children's
Book of the
Eclipse, '99,
Moon's Special
Day". To produce
bright, exciting
illustrations to
compliment text by
Caroline
Stephenson for 3-8
year olds

title
White Horses
medium
Dr Marten's, inks,
mono-printing
purpose of work
Children's book for
3-5 year olds

brief
To illustrate my
own text "White
Horses" to inspire
children's
imaginations with
bold colour and
rhythm

natalie bärthel

2 Norfolk Road
Falmouth
Cornwall
TR11 3NT
t. 01326 319417
f. 01326 212033
m. 0780 845 1301
email.natalie.baerth
el@talk21.com

title
Audubon's Watch
medium
Digital / Photoshop
purpose of work
Book jacket design
(live brief)
brief
Create a striking
image for the
unpublished novel
"Audubon's Watch"
by John Gregory
Brown
Commissioned by
AD Ian Hughes
Company
Hodder &
Stoughton Book
Publishers

Idea - based
illustrator working
in any medium to
suit requirements
of given brief

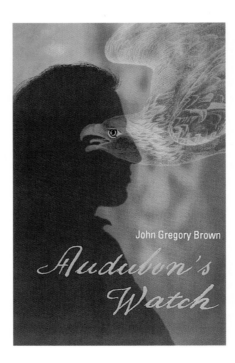

10 Radley Drive
Nuneaton
Warwickshire
CV10 7HX

t. 024 7634 6811
f. 07801 546404

title
Where Do I Come
From?

medium
Mixed Media

purpose of work
Student project
brief

brief
To create an
imaginative
response to
questions asked
about the body

title
How Big is my
Heart?

medium
Mixed Media

purpose of work
Student project
brief

brief
To create an
imaginative
response to
questions asked
concerning the
body

jennette white

1 Neston Road
Walshaw
Bury
Lancashire
BL8 3DB

t. 01204 883167
f. 01204 883167

title
Catching Stars

medium
Acrylic

purpose of work
Children's Book

brief
To write a
children's story and
produce
accompanying
illustrations

Illustration by Frank Love +44 (0)20 8297 2212

Janie Markham / Commissioning Editor / The Art Group

Andrew Coningsby / Agent & Gallery Proprietor

Adrian Johnson / Illustrator

judges   **Paul Webster** / Art Director / Sainsbury Magazine

unpublished

Unpublished

Section winner: Belle Mellor Wrapping Paper
Design process by Anna Steinberg

The Unpublished section always receives a high number of entries and fulfils a variety of purposes. Significantly it is a platform to show clients the range of an artist's talents without alarming them with a radical departure from the norm mid-commission. It also serves as a waiting room for the illustration world where the editor-worrying controversies, design triumphs that clients pulled the budget on and general imagery good, bad and ugly gets a second shot at glory.

It is the third consecutive year that Belle has had work accepted into the Unpublished section with self promotional work. She says it is often this work that comes to mind when choosing her entries for *Images*. In 1997 her pantomime cow Christmas card to clients was accepted into the book as was a return from travelling mailout in 1998. Those, and this year's unpublished section winner, *Wrapping Paper* have elicited positive responses both from clients that received them initially as well as impressing the judging panel.

Belle's mailouts are produced small scale and low tech and succeed through being fun and memorable to receive. This marketing strategy extends to sticking chocolate money to her invoices, a public relations coup that British Telecom have yet to get wise to. Her *Wrapping Paper* is compiled from several sketchbooks worth of doodles created in inspired moments over the past year.

Belle's first commission was from Tatler and the bulk of her clients since then have been editorial, with the odd design, advertising and publishing job thrown in for good measure. Belle graduated from Bath College with a first in 1994 and her work since then has been constant.

belle mellor

Flat 3
12 Lansdowne
Street
Hove
East Sussex
BN3 1FQ

t. 01273 732604
f. 01273 732604
m. 0973 463 942

189

GB

title
Wrapping Paper
medium
Pen and ink
purpose of work
Self promotional
wrapping paper

agent
Three in a Box Inc
468 Queen Street
East
#104 Box 03
Toronto on Msaitt
Canada
t. 001 416 367 2446

michael bramman

104 Dudley Court
Upper Berkeley
Street
London
W1H 7PJ

t. 020 7723 3564
f. 020 7723 3564

★ **winner:** *Daler and Rowney*
- best use of traditional materials

DALER~ROWNEY
TRUSTED *by* ARTISTS WORLDWIDE

190
GB

title
A Little Tram Music

medium
Acrylic

purpose of work
Personal

brief
Promotional

paul catherall

16D Lordship Park
Stoke Newington
London
N16 5UD

t. 020 8809 1574
t. 020 7207 3031
f. 020 8809 1574

title
Oxo Tower
medium
Oil based lino-print
purpose of work
Self promotional
brief
One of a series of
prints based on
architecture in
London

agent
The Art Market
27 Old Gloucester
Street
London
WC1N 3AF
t. 020 7209 1123

title
Castro Cigars
medium
Oil based lino-print
purpose of work
Self promotional
brief
Packaging
illustration for
imaginary cigar
pack

agent
The Art Market
27 Old Gloucester
Street
London
WC1N 3AF
t. 020 7209 1123

russell cobb

Monster
The Studio, St. Bridgets
Radcliffe Road, Hitchin
Hertfordshire, SG5 1QH

t. 01462 441614
f. 01462 441614
m. 0961 414 613
email. russellcobb@hotmail.com

title
New Collection,
Autumnal Range

medium
Acrylic

purpose of work
Promotional card

brief
One of a series of
promotional cards
designed to show
different elements
of the illustrators
work

mike davidson

79 Granville Park
London
SE13 7DW

t. 020 8318 1169

title
Madison Square

medium
Radiograph pens,
airbrushed inks and
gouache

purpose of work
Personal work

brief
To convey the
colour and
business of the
street contrasted
with the calm and
geometry of the
buildings

cecilia eales

14 High Road
Ickenham
Middlesex
UB10 8LJ

t. 01895 634941
f. 01895 634941
m. 07939 335 287

194
GB

UNPUBLISHED

title
Chinatown

medium
Crayon and
photocopier

purpose of work
Personal work

brief
To document
personal
experience of New
York

cecilia eales

14 High Road
Ickenham
Middlesex
UB10 8LJ

t. 01895 634941
f. 01895 634941
m. 07939 335 287

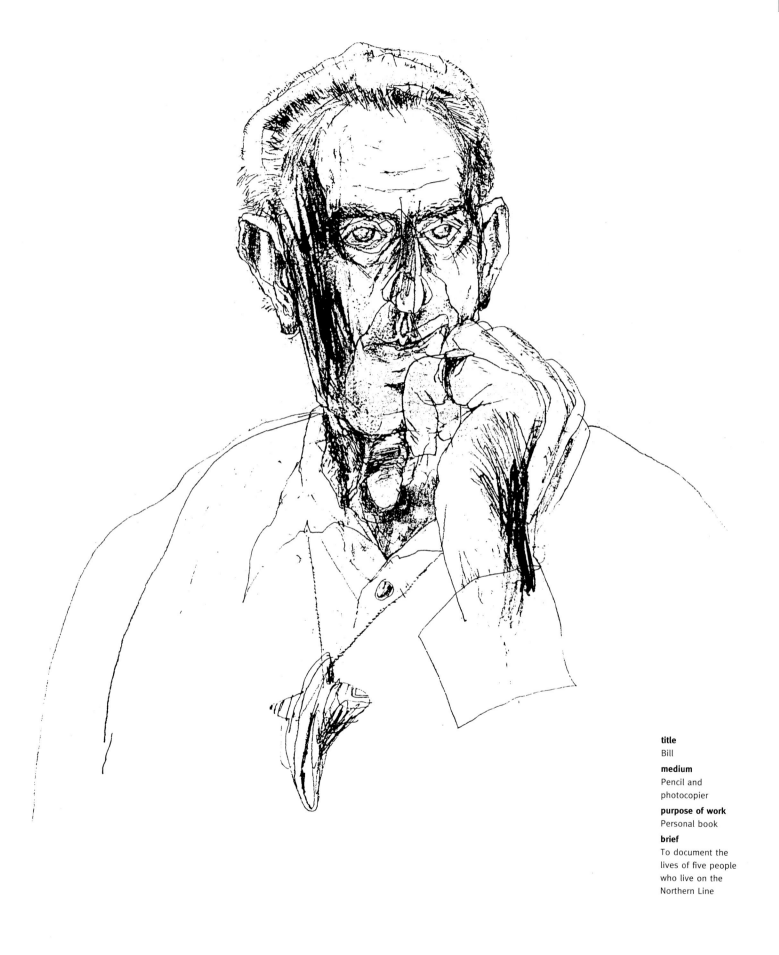

title
Bill

medium
Pencil and
photocopier

purpose of work
Personal book

brief
To document the
lives of five people
who live on the
Northern Line

kevin hauff

7 Pendre Avenue
Prestatyn
Denbighshire
LL19 9SH

t. 01745 888734
f. 01745 888734

title
Go On! Be a Devil

medium
Acrylic and collage

purpose of work
Self Promotional

brief
One of a series of humorous images exploring the concept of temptation, in response to the copy line - "Is it Good to be Bad?"

christine farrell

9 Lochy Place
Erskine
Renfrewshire
Scotland
PA8 6AY

t. 0141 812 4431
f. 01382 201378
email. c.m.z.farrell@dundee.ac.uk

197
GB

title
Granny Allen's
Bottom Drawer

medium
Mixed media with
wooden spoon

purpose of work
Personal work

brief
To convey the
humour of the
following statement
by Granny Allen: "If
I had known what
your grandpa was
going to do to me
that night, there'd
have been no
wedding!"

richard hejsak

Ricamona Studios
11 Kendalls Close
High Wycombe
Buckinghamshire
HP13 7NN

t. 01494 531 117
email. ricamona@studios11.freeserve.co.uk

198

GB

title
What to Wear?

medium
Gouache and
crayon

purpose of work
Speculative
editorial piece

brief
Produce an
illustration for an
editorial fashion
spread entitled
"Summer Trends,
What to Wear?"

title
Sunday Afternoon
Scrum
medium
Watercolour
purpose of work
Speculative

agent
Arena
144 Royal College
Street
London
NW1 0TA
t. 020 7267 9661

title
Sunday Cricketer
medium
Watercolour
purpose of work
Speculative
brief
Cricket to appeal to
the amateur (for
possible use on
limited edition
prints)

agent
Arena
144 Royal College
Street
London
NW1 0TA
t. 020 7267 9661

alison lang

Flat A
37 Drewstead Road
London
SW16 1LY

t. 020 8677 8889
f. 020 8677 8889
m. 07932 680 362
email. alison.lang@tesco.net

title
Two Fat Ladies
medium
Watercolour
purpose of work
Self Promotional
brief
To show two great
personalities in all
their splendour

satoshi kambayashi

Flat 2
40 Tisbury Road
Hove
East Sussex
BN3 3BA

t. 01273 771539
f. 01273 771539
email. satoshi.k@virgin.net

title
Danger, Direct and
Passive

medium
Line and wash

purpose of work
Self promotional

brief
Create an image to
illustrate a danger
posed by smoking

agent
Ian Flemming &
Associates
t. 020 7734 8701

tiffany lynch

Flat 4
41 Islington Park Street
London
N1 1QB

t. 020 7704 8454
m. 07711 340 434
email. tiffany@moose.co.uk

title
Green Bottle and
Olives

medium
Acrylic

purpose of work
Personal design

brief
To produce a
pleasing design:
part of a collection
of still lifes. A
personal project

agent
New Division
32 Shelton Street
Covent Garden
London
WC2H 9HP
t. 020 7497 2555

ian massey

12 Gloucester Avenue
Levenshulme
Manchester
M19 3WT
t. 0161 224 0079
email. ian@masmot.demon.co.uk

title
Night Bird Cantata
medium
Mixed media on
paper
purpose of work
Self promotion for
exhibition &
portfolio (one of a
series)

brief
To produce a series
of pieces based
upon a reading of
"The Night Bird
Cantata" by Donald
Rawley

ben mccaffrey

47 Campbell Road
Maidstone
Kent
ME15 6PY
t. 01622 764481

title
Children of the
Red Star

medium
Acrylic and
gouache

purpose of work
Personal

brief
To illustrate novel
"Wild Swans" by
Jung Chang

katharine mcewen

520 Clerkenwell Workshops
31 Clerkenwell Close
London
EC1R 0AT

t. 020 7490 3315
f. 020 7490 3315
pager. 01426 229 029

title
Sock it to the
Monkey

medium
Watercolour &
pencil crayon

purpose of work
Self promotional

brief
To illustrate an
article warning
office-goers against
the hazards of
wearing too short
socks under a suit
thus revealing
horrible monkey
legs

julie monks

42 Fenwick Road
London
SE15 4HW

t. 020 7252 9243
f. 020 7252 9243
m. 07930 347 016

title
He liked to Drive
into Town
medium
Oil Paint
purpose of work
Personal promotion

agent
Peter's, Fraser &
Dunlop
Drury House
34-43 Russell
Street
London
WC2B 5HA
t. 020 7344 1000

title
Show Business is
Dog Eat Dog
medium
Oil Paint
purpose of work
Personal promotion

agent
Peter's, Fraser &
Dunlop
Drury House
34-43 Russell
Street
London
WC2B 5HA
t. 020 7344 1000

title
He Had an Idea
medium
Oil Paint
purpose of work
Personal promotion

agent
Peter's, Fraser &
Dunlop
Drury House
34-43 Russell
Street
London
WC2B 5HA
t. 020 7344 1000

shane mcgowan

23a Parkholme Road
London
E8 3AG

t. 020 7249 6444
f. 020 7249 6444
email. shane.mcgowan@virgin.net

title
Peace of Mind

medium
Gouache and ink

purpose of work
To illustrate article
about illness
insurance

brief
Do something
"Blindingly simple"

commissioned by
Andrew Chapman

company
Moneywise
Magazine

agent
The Organisation
69 Caledonian
Road
London
N1 9BT
t. 020 7833 8268

mario minichiello

61 Scotland Road
Little Bowden
Market Harborough
Leicestershire
LE16 8AY

t. 01858 431456
f. 01858 431456
m. 07932 425872
email. mariom@globalnet.co.uk

title
Zio e Zia

medium
Ink

purpose of work
Book of travels in
southern Italy

brief
Work produced for
a book illustrating
travels around
southern Italy, its
people, places and
customs

WINSOR & NEWTON
The World's Finest Artists' Materials

★ **winner:** *The Windsor & Newton Award*

liz minichiello

61 Scotland Road
Little Bowden
Market Harborough
Leicestershire
LE16 8AY

t. 01858 431456

title
St Martins Place
medium
Gouache and ink
purpose of work
Self promotional
brief
One of a series of
images depicting
aspects of London

award winner

title
Campaign to
promote Allotments
medium
Gouache
purpose of work
To illustrate
government report

brief
To enliven the
social and
environmental
benefits of
gardening on an
allotment

pierre-paul pariseau

3997 St Dominique St., 2
Montreal
Quebec, Canada
H2W 2A4

t. 001 514 849 2964
f. 001 514 843 4808

title
1. The Joy of Sex
2. Book Birds
3. Natural Envy

medium
Photo collage

purpose of work
Promotional
pictures

agent
The Organisation
69 Caledonian Rd
Kings Cross
London N1 9BT
t. 020 7833 8268

peter mundee

Courtyard Studio
Panther House
38 Mount Pleasant
London
WC1X 0AP

t. 020 7833 4113
f. 020 7833 3064
m. 0976 353 677

title
Joke Shop
medium
Acrylic
purpose of work
Self promotional

agent
C.I.A.
36 Wellington
Street
London
WC2E 7BD
t. 020 7240 8925

UNPUBLISHED

garry parsons

212

GB

249 Bellenden
Road
London
SE15 4DQ

t. 020 7358 1856
m. 07931 923 934

title
Chattanooga
medium
Acrylic
purpose of work
Collaborative book
project
brief
Illustration for the
song "Chattanooga
Choo Choo"

richard myers

13 Cavendish Avenue
Harrogate
North Yorkshire
HG2 8HX

t. 01423 504172

UNPUBLISHED

title
To the River

medium
Paint and collage

purpose of work
Double page
spread from
Cambridge book

brief
To illustrate a book
about Cambridge
entitled "A Day
around the City"

chris robson

13 Whatley Road
Clifton
Bristol
BS8 2PS

t. 0117 973 7694
f. 0117 973 7694
mobile. 0797 137 9354
email. cbrobson@aol.com

214

GB

title
Cars and Drivers

medium
Brush and ink

purpose of work
Design company
pitch for Ford

brief
Funky people in
funky cars

commissioned by
Mik Baines

company
Firehouse

charlotte powell

71 Cardigan Terrace
Heaton
Newcastle-upon-Tyne
NE6 5NX

t. 0191 276 2071

215
GB

title
Rub A Dub Dub
medium
Oil on Board
purpose of work
Experimental - Self
Promotional

brief
To illustrate the
children's nursery
rhyme "Rub A Dub
Dub"

title
Orlando
medium
Beads, gems, lace
and oil on canvas
purpose of work
Experimental - Self
Promotional
brief
To illustrate
Virginia Woolf's
novel "Orlando"

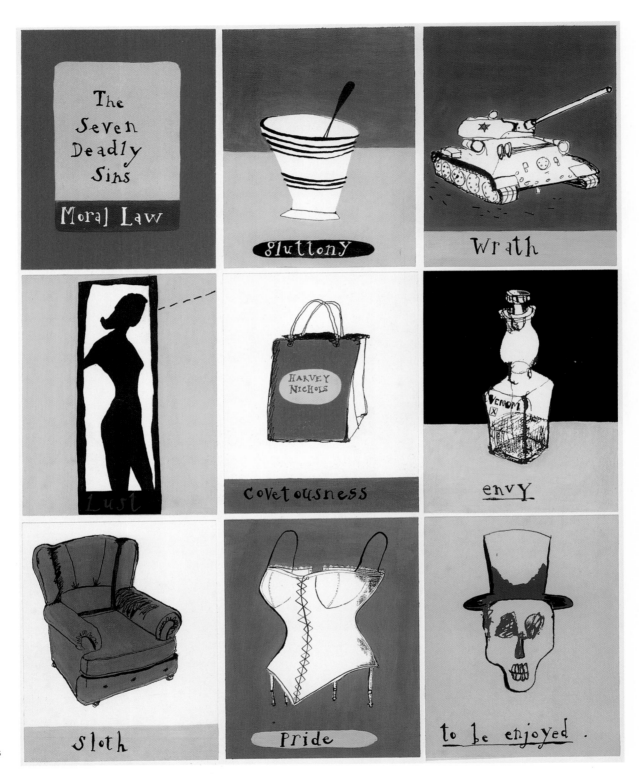

title
The Seven
Deadly Sins

medium
Pen and ink and
acrylic

purpose of work
Self promotional

brief
To illustrate the
seven deadly sins
in a fun, quirky,
way

agent
The Inkshed
98 Columbia Road
London
E2 7QB
t. 020 7613 2323

anna steinberg

6 Langler Road
London
NW10 5TL

t. 020 8964 1069
f. 020 8964 1069
pager. 01426 355 030

title
Backgammon

medium
Biro

purpose of work
Holiday sketchbook

jonathan williams

4A Addison Drive
Littlemore
Oxford
OX4 3UD
t. 01865 747364
f. 01865 747364
m. 07867 526477
email. blazing.fruit@btinternet.com

218
GB

title
Street Preacher

medium
Photoshop

purpose of work
Experimental

brief
As time goes by,
the end is not as
close as it used
to be

jonathan williams

4A Addison Drive
Littlemore
Oxford
OX4 3UD
t. 01865 747364
f. 01865 747364
m. 07867 526477
email. blazing.fruit@btinternet.com

title
Chain Smoker at
the White Tower

medium
Photoshop

purpose of work
Experimental

brief
A visual fragment
from a visit to
Thessaloniki,
Greece

sara hayward

Four Seasons
Battenhall Avenue
Worcester
WR5 2HW

t. 01905 357563
f. 01905 357563

title
Cala San Vincente

medium
Acrylic

purpose of work
For exhibitions

brief
A series of colour
studies capturing
the changing light
of a view from a
balcony

simon welch

209 Church Road
Bexleyheath
Kent
DA7 4DU

t. 020 8304 1176
m. 07932 674954

title
Blue Bell
medium
Mixed, inc plaster
purpose of work
Personal project

AOI membership benefits & costs

Membership of the AOI is open to all illustrators, illustration students, agents, lecturers and illustration clients.

All categories of membership receive the following benefits:

- Monthly journal
- Discounted rate at events
- Discounted rate for *Images* – call for entries, hanging fees and annual pages
- Contact details on office database for enquiries from clients
- Access to the portfolio insurance scheme
- Portfolio stickers
- Discounts from material suppliers
- Regional group contacts
- Purchase of artwork stickers

In addition we provide the following services for particular types of membership:–

Full Membership

This category is for professional illustrators who have had work commissioned and accept the AOI code of conduct.

- Legal advice on contracts and book publishing agreements
- Hotline information on pricing and professional practice
- Free annual portfolio surgery
- Reduced rate account with couriers
- Invitation to the *Images* private view
- Discounted rate on selected hotel accommodation in London
- Purchase of editorial, publishing and advertising directories
- Business advice – an hour's free consultation with a chartered accountant on accounts, book–keeping, National Insurance, VAT and tax
- Full members are entitled to use the affix 'Mem AOI'
- Full members are supplied with a list of agents and advice about agents

Associate Membership

This one-year category is for newcomers and illustrators on their first year out of college who have not published work. In exceptional circumstances this membership can be extended.

- Hotline information on pricing and professional practice
- Free annual portfolio surgery
- Discounted rate on selected hotel accommodation in London
- Purchase of editorial and publishing directories
- Business advice – an hour's free consultation with a chartered accountant on accounts, book-keeping, National Insurance, VAT and tax.

Student membership

This service is for students on full-time illustration or related courses

- See above services for all AOI members

Corporate Membership

This service is for agents and clients from the illustration industry

- Free copy of the *Images* catalogue
- All corporate members' staff and illustrators will receive discounts on events and *Images*

For an application form and cost details contact:

Association of Illustrators
1-5 Beehive Place
London SW9 7QR
Tel: +44 (0)20 7733 5844
Fax: +44 (0)20 7733 1199
E-mail: info@a-o-illustrators.demon.co.uk
Website: www.aoi.co.uk

College Membership

College membership entitles the college to the following benefits:

- A free lecture from an AOI Council Member or selected illustrator on the creative, ethical and business aspects of illustration.
- Free copy of *Images* annual
- AOI monthly Journal

RONALD SEARLE

AOI publications

Survive: The illustrators Guide to a Professional Career

Published by the AOI, *Survive* is the only comprehensive and in-depth guide to illustration as a professional career. Established illustrators, agents, clients and a range of other professionals have contributed to this fourth edition. Each area of the profession including portfolio presentation, self promotion and copyright issues are looked at in detail. The wealth of information in *Survive* makes it absolutely indispensable to the newcomer and also has much to offer the more experienced illustrator.

Rights: The illustrators Guide to Professional Practice

Rights is an all inclusive guide to aspects of the law specifically related to illustration. It includes information about copyright, contracts, book publishing agreements, agency agreements, advice about seeking legal advice, how to calculate fees and guidance on how to write a licence.

Rights is the result of a number of years of research. It has been approved by solicitors and contains the most detailed and accurate model terms and conditions available for use by illustrators or clients.

www.aoi.co.uk

AOI website

Gallery

A showcase for illustrator's work. Regularly updated, the Gallery now contains hundreds of images that are easily searchable by name, style, subject, keyword etc. Images are initially viewed as thumbnails with the artists' name providing a link to their contact details and biography. Users have the option of saving selected images, together with any written comments, to a private folder. Additionally, two or more users can set up a shared image folder with its own password.

News

Up to date industry news is regularly recorded. News archives are searchable by year, month and keyword. Users who wish to be e-mailed the latest industry news as it appears on the site can select this option when logging on (located in the Chat area).

Magazine

The Association's monthly magazine on-line. Archives contain a wealth of material fully searchable by keyword.

Chat

The place to post your thoughts and enter discussion on any topics of concern to the illustration community.

Info

General information about the AOI including a full list of services, events, publications and membership.

Other Features

Personal Web Address
Illustrators appearing on the site can have a personal web address linked directly to their images.

Postcards
Any chosen image from the Gallery can be mailed together with a message as an electronic 'postcard'.

I-mail
A secure internal e-mail system for users to contact each other

The site is open to all areas of the illustration community. Illustrators or agents wishing to submit images to the Gallery can find complete details on-line or by telephoning the AOI office.

AOI on-line has been developed for the Association of Illustrators by Warp Interactive.

Contact Tim Deighton at Warp on +44 (0)20 7978 9868 or the AOI on +44 (0)20 7733 5844

Index